Alexandria's Light

Women's Devotional Workbook

To: HARLI-
continue w/
the journey
of what God has
for you - Enjoy
alexandria's
Light as
you.

A. Nicole Strom'

Dedication

I dedicate this book to three strong women who loved me unconditionally - my beloved mother, Monica Rency Johnson Smith, my great aunt, Arnetta "Aunt Peaches" Winkfield Hill, and my grandmother, Stella Winkfield Smith, who have all gone on to be with our Heavenly Father. You are all missed dearly.

Acknowledgements

Special thanks to my Lord and Savior Jesus Christ for using me as an instrument in the birthing of *Alexandria's Light*. Many thanks go to my husband, Rob, who is the absolute love of my life, and our sons, Alexander and Keagan, for their unconditional love and support. To my father, Doug, the photographer - thank you for your continuous support through my life's journey. To my brother, Doug II - thank you for always being in my corner and for continuing the close relationship we have, even in our adult lives. To an awesome woman, my mother-in-law, Pat, I thank God for you and the relationship we have; thank you for your courage, honesty, love and support. To my aunt and uncle, Gary and Wanda Brown, thank you for your countless acts of generosity, godly counsel, kindness and genuine love for me and my family throughout the years. To our pastor, Willis G. Polk I and our church family at Imani Church, thank you for grooming me and preparing me spiritually for this project. To the best group of co-workers I could ever have - you all are amazing women. And to the one God used to name this book, I thank you for being obedient in delivering the message.

Last, but certainly not least, I want to thank my editor, Charliese Brown Lewis, for believing in me, working with me, and pushing me to greater heights. I cannot thank you enough. You are truly a blessing to me. I thank God for putting us on the same paths all these years.

Foreword

Last year, Nicole Stromberg shared with me that she was writing a devotional book. I asked her, "What is this book going to be about?" She began to share her thoughts about the vision that God had given her to help women of God. I have known Nicole our entire lives and I never knew her to be a writer. I remember watching her struggle in school with the learning disability, Dyslexia. Back then, there were so many misconceptions about it. Having this reading disorder did not mean she was not smart; it just meant that she processed things differently than others. I would later understand that what many considered a disability would ultimately be God manifesting a spiritual gift in her that would be probably less understood than the disability itself.

As she began to talk about this book from day to day, I let her know that if she was really serious, I would come on board as her editor because I truly believed in her vision for this project, but I certainly saw God working in her more and more in our conversations. I told her that it would be a grueling process, often frustrating, and certainly time consuming. Honestly, I had no idea what I had signed up for either. But I knew that God had put us on a path to "write the vision and make it plain" for women who were just like us.

At our first meeting, we sat down at her dining room table with large posted notepaper on her walls, highlighters, pens, pencils, erasers, a computer, and an LCD projector. We, along with her husband, outlined the project and her thoughts. We scrapped the entire first outline just days after we had invested numerous hours in the process. Then we started over. Eventually, we got to where we are today, but it took us some time.

Alexandria's Light is Nicole's personal journey that gives life to her experiences with her students, clients, prayer partners, family members, friends, but most of all, God. As women, some of our stories are similar. We all have experiences that put us in a place where we feel like we have lost all hope, but also that God cannot use us for His glory. We are not all at a place where we see God's light inside of us. But the Word of God declares:

"You are the light of the world. A town built on a hill cannot be hidden. Neither do people light a lamp and put it under a bowl. Instead they put it on its stand, and it gives light to everyone in the house. In the same way, let your light shine before others, that they may see your good deeds and glorify your Father in heaven" (Matthew 5:14-16, NIV version).

Maybe someone is struggling with depression. Perhaps someone is in an ~ relationship. Maybe someone is on the verge of suicide. Perhaps some~ physically unattractive. I promise that the reader will find a resembl~

personal story as she turns the pages of this book. *Alexandria's Light* is purposely written and edited in Nicole's authentic voice as if she is speaking personally to the reader. The grammar and punctuation even reflect the cadence in her voice. It is a bold approach to addressing each reader personally. It is a brave approach to expressing her story to help others desire more of God.

Just like our journey together to get to this point, this book will take readers on an unexpected, spiritual journey of self-discovery. There will certainly be laughter, tears, frustration, stretching, learning and growing. I have no doubt that God's plan for your life will be revealed through this literary ministry, but mostly, this devotional workbook will show someone the beauty of God's marvelous light that lives on the inside. Enjoy the journey.

Charliese Brown Lewis
Co-author of *The 'After Church' Experience* blog

Introduction

Alexandria's Light means "hope". It is focused on the hope in finding the light of Jesus Christ that flows from Him to us, through this written and inspired Women's Devotional Workbook. The "light" of this book will give hope to the hopeless or hope to someone who may need a little encouragement. For women who desire a closer relationship with our Heavenly Father, this devotional was especially designed for the "Daughters of Christ".

Hello, Reader!

1Corinthians 14:40 says that we are supposed to do all things in decency and in order, just like the order of the church. So, I wanted to give the readers a bit of direction for *Alexandria's Light Devotional Workbook.*

This is a 52-week devotional workbook geared toward helping women develop a closer relationship with the Lord through intimate, personal and quiet time. Each week will take the reader on a five-day journey of reflections and devotional work. The other two days are for each person to meditate or catch up on the days, keeping in mind that life is busy, but there must be sacrifices made to get closer to God.

You, the reader, are to read the devotional at the top of the page each day and do the workbook assignment for each designated day. I recommend you take your time with each day. The main purpose is for you to get all that God has intended for you to get out of this devotional workbook and to consider in what ways you can apply it to your daily living. The end goal is for your relationship with God to become closer and for your desire for Him to increase.

You will need the following items to ensure your success on this journey: a notebook or a personal journal, pen or pencil, and your favorite highlighter. These items will help you with your responses and for the activities in the book.

Through *Alexandria's Light*, I pray you get all the healing, deliverance and victory that God has waiting for you!

When Jesus spoke again to the people, he said, "I am the light of the world. Whoever follows me will never walk in darkness, but will have the light of life" (John 8:12).

Be blessed as you begin this journey. Welcome to the light.

John 1:1-5 (NKJV)

1 In the beginning was the Word, and the Word was with God, and the Word was God. 2 He was in the beginning with God. 3 All things were made through Him, and without Him nothing was made that was made. 4 In Him was life, and the life was the light of men. 5 And the light shines in the darkness, and darkness did not comprehend it.

THE WORD IN THE BEGINNING

As I was putting the final touches on *Alexandria's Light*, the Lord dropped in my spirit that I didn't have a proper beginning for the book. I was hitting the pavement right off but, without a proper beginning. In order to have an orderly book I needed to have a beginning since I already had an ending. It's like having the dash on the tombstone that signifies the time that exists between birth and death. What was I to put in front of the dash to begin the journey? That would be like having a project or an event that had no start date, but had an end date. For this book that would look like a dash followed by 52 for the weekly devotionals or it could be the start date and an end date for this book. It would look like 2012-2015. I began to talk with the Lord. I asked Him questions as to how He wanted me to do this; I felt such a pressing in my spirit, which led me to John 1:1-5. After some reflection, the Spirit moved me through all of these devotional entries.

Just as I have given you instruction for a strong foundation for this devotional book a few pages back, I believe that is what John is telling us about this Scripture. He was saying: in the beginning was the Word, which is the law of God and everything made was done by God alone. He didn't need our help in creating this world. He said that in Him was life, the light of men, Jesus, who walked this earth in the form of a human being. The light that shines in darkness, which the darkness could not understand it, is Jesus who shines through us all. We must remember that without God, there would be no creation of any kind. Let me remind you of who we really are.

As children of the light, we are no longer in darkness as God sent His only son to die for our sins. It's time we start acting like we are "Daughters of Light" and stop walking around in doom and gloom. No more ladies! Ecclesiastes 3:1 (NKJV) says, to everything there is a season, a time for every purpose under the heaven. Let's keep that in mind as you go through the journey of *Alexandria's Light Devotional Workbook*. This is your time to get healed, time for you to be delivered, and time for you to be set free from emotional stress, financial burdens, depression, and the list goes on and on. Make a commitment to go all the way through this journey – to the very end. Receive and begin to walk in what God has for you. Even after you complete this devotional workbook, continue on your life journey with Christ. You will be surprised at how it will completely change your life forever…

WORKBOOK ENTRY #1 *Jan. 6th, 2016*

DAY 1

Describe what the beginning of your day is like. Do you start it off in the Word?

Not usually. I hate waking up early. I can be lazy. we're on a media fast right now. It's a wake up call.

How does your day end usually, in the Word, in prayer, in quiet reflection? Explain.

Most of the time, I try. I'm a night owl so this works best for me.

DAY 2

Who is the "light of men"? Why was He sent?

Jesus is. Obviously. He was sent to be the ultimate sacrifice for our sin. To prove His love, even though He didn't need to.

Whose light shines in darkness? How do you know?

God's / Jesus / Holy Spirits. I've seen it. Being at DQ right now; working with who I work with... It's difficult to be a light. But God always shows up.

In what form did Jesus walk this earth?

He walked this Earth in the flesh. All man, all God.

DAY 3

Who does Jesus' light shine through? What is the evidence?

I would say His light shines through His people. The evidence is probably how they live their life.

As children of the light, what are we no longer a part of? Why?

We're no longer a part of the world. Why should we want to be? There's only temporary happiness in that.

How do you allow His light to shine through you? Explain.

I try my best to be an open and willing vessel. To let Him use me. For my name not to be known/seen... but His.

DAY 4

Read all of Chapter 3 in Ecclesiastes. Write down your interpretation of this chapter.

Ecclesiastes 3 explains how time is so important to us. As you go through the journey of *Alexandria's Light* write down your goals as to what you would like to see happen this year - just as if you would if you were doing your New Year's resolutions. Keep a written journal of all your experiences and things you want to overcome while you complete this devotional workbook. But first, start by listing your realistic expectations you want to overcome. List a few below and make your request plan.

1.

2.

3.

4.

5.

DAY 5

PRAYING TIME!

All wise God, your Word declares that the Word was the Word, and the Word was with God, and the Word was God. I am praying that the Word that goes forth in this devotional workbook will shine through to all that read it. Thank you for your Word, Lord. May it go far and do much for your daughters. May it reach each woman to the very depths of her being. May His Word, His love, and His light, live in you. As you go on your journey may your light begin to shine, just like Jesus' light shines. In the precious name of Jesus I pray. Amen, Amen and Amen.

1 Peter 3:3 (Amplified)
Do not let your adornment be merely outward - arranging the hair, wearing gold, or putting on fine apparel

MEASURING UP

The Bible says that Peter is trying to give instructions to the wives for their husbands regarding their outward appearance. He was telling us that yes it is okay to look good on the outside, but let's really deal with what is on the inside – the inner most of our being – what God wants us to have shine through for others to see.

In today's time, it is really hard for women to just see ourselves as the complete package because of what society says we should do and be. We worry about measuring up to others or just trying to make ourselves feel good. We, as women, like to look good. But this is not what Peter is saying to us. He is asking what are we doing to let our lives show the Christ in us.

So many times I have tried to measure up to all the fashion standards and our society by conforming to the world's standard of beauty. But if we look at what Peter has instructed – God is who we should be pleasing first – before we try to please others and measure up to their standards. Let your sons, daughters, friends and family see the Christ in you way before they see all the things that sparkle and glitter. Ask the Lord to show you what you can do to please Him *first*. He searches our hearts to see our inner beauty.

WORKBOOK ENTRY #2

DAY 1

What does this Scripture tell you about how God sees us?

_____

Circle 3 of the words below that resemble how God wants you to be *outwardly*.

Loud/Boastful   Inner Beauty
Gentle & Quite Spirit   Defiant/Disobedient
Pleasing to Man   Pleasing to Him

DAY 2

- Read 1Thessalonians 2:4
- Read Acts 5:29

What do these two Scriptures have in common?

_____

Who should we trust and who should we please?

_____

DAY 3

How have you tried to measure up to man's standards? How far has it gotten you?

_____
_____
_____

What do you find beautiful about yourself?

_____
_____
_____

What do you believe God finds beautiful about you?

_____
_____
_____

DAY 4

Scripture tells us not to trust _man_ but, to trust _God._

What steps will you take to start pleasing God first?

_____
_____
_____

Circle your answer Yes or No.

1. Will you spend more time in His Word? Yes/No
2. Will you stop seeking man's approval? Yes/No
3. Will you trust God and believe in His word? Yes/No

DAY 5

PRAYING TIME!

Pray this prayer:

Lord, may I only look to you to feel special. May I put my trust in you and not in man. May I look into my inner being and feel your gentle spirit upon me. May I look to your standards instead of trying to meet society's standards. In Jesus' name I pray, Amen!

1Chronicles 16:29 (NKJV)
...Oh worship the Lord in the beauty of holiness...

EYES OF THE BEHOLDER

When you think about beauty, you probably think about the look of something or the look of somebody. We often think people are beautiful because of their physical looks, their smiles, or maybe their hair; so many *other* things than what beauty really is. When we think of holiness, we think of purity, sacredness, or even goodness. All of these adjectives describe people and things. As a child of God, we should look at our beauty just as Christ looks at worship - being pure and good. When we worship we should not worry about what we look like, because it shall all be unto God.

There has been so many times that I have gone to church wanting to do nothing but worship God, but couldn't. The pastor gives you permission to do so and you don't. I always seem to wonder what I will look like, if people are going to stare, or how ugly my facial expressions are going to be. I think about all the wrong things. When we worship we should only be concerned with worship to God - glorifying Him for all that He has done for us and all that He is about to do in our lives - in the lives of our family members, on our jobs, with our children and with our health. We should worship God as it says "in spirit and in truth". Never be ashamed or embarrassed to praise God by yourself or in a room full of people. Forget about what other people think about you worshiping and praising God – just get *your* best praise on!

Ever since I have stopped worrying about what my fellow church members might think, as a result my worship has become more authentic and a lot bolder. I finally feel like the bondage has been lifted off of me. Every time I raise my hands, I feel my release, my freedom to worship. I feel all types of blessings coming down. This is why I say, "Forget about what other people think about your worship and praise!" Go ahead and do it any way.

To God Be the Glory.

Just for a few minutes, worship God and not worry about what it looks like.

WORKBOOK ENTRY #3

DAY 1

Define what beauty means to you?

_____

How does your definition line up with the Scripture?

_____
_____
_____

DAY 2

Practice worshiping God. Remember, your body is the first instrument of praise. Use your hands to clap. Use your arms to wave your hands. Use your feet to stomp the devil out. Incorporate your song, music, dance and any instrument you are gifted to play. Now that you have attempted to worship in the comfort of your own home, challenge yourself and do it at church. Don't worry about what you look like or be concerned with who is watching you. God is the only one that matters. Focus your eyes on Him. JUST GIVE GOD THE PRAISE!

DAY 3

Read Psalm 150

Write down how David worshiped God. How does your praise resemble David's praise?

_____
_____
_____

Complete this sentence: Let _____ that has _____ praise the Lord! Praise The Lord! Psalm 150:6.

DAY 4

What instruction is God speaking to you about worshiping Him?

_____

_____

_____

What does He want you to use to praise Him? *Clue: Look back at Day 3 to check your answer.

_____

The next time you are in the House of Worship, try using some of the examples of worship mentioned in Day 3.

DAY 5

PRAYING TIME!

Pray and ask God to remove all the apprehension you may have about worshiping Him in public.

Write your prayer down.

_____

_____

_____

My prayer for you:

Gracious Father, we thank you for giving us instructions as to how you want us to worship you. May you remove all fears that might hinder me from praising you with all that I have! May I be able to give you, Lord, all the praise, the glory and honor that is due you. It's in Jesus' precious name I pray, Amen.

Proverbs 31:10 (Amplified)
...she is worth far more than rubies

INSIDE OUT

When you read today's devotional Bible verse, it should make you excited! To know that we are more than all the material things in this world is so important! What a blessing to know that we are worth more than any piece of clothing, jewelry or even a car. I know you are saying, "These things make me". When I was younger, I would often wonder why I wasn't as shapely or as tall as my friends. Then I began to appreciate my weight and my height as I got older.

Well, I challenge you today to love yourself for the other qualities you have: your intelligence, your beauty inside and out (whether you want to believe it or not), and even your creativity. It is important that you learn to love and appreciate yourself just the way you are. When you learn to love you, then others will love you the way you deserve to be loved in return.

Look in the mirror today and say three times, "I AM FABULOUS!"
Because you are…

WORKBOOK ENTRY #4

DAY 1

In Proverbs 31:10, underline the word(s) that make you important.

How do you describe your worth as a woman? Does it reflect anything in this passage?

DAY 2

Read Proverbs 31:10-31 – The Virtuous Woman

In your own words, describe what she looks like.

_____

_____

_____

Describe her role as the woman of her house. How important is her role in her home?

_____

_____

_____

DAY 3

Did you know you are just as important as the Virtuous Woman?

List three things you have in common with her based on the Scripture.

    1. _____

    2. _____

    3. _____

Name one of your own personal strengths that resemble one of hers.

_____

_____

_____

DAY 4

Look in the mirror today and say out loud, "I AM FABULOUS!"

Tell yourself out loud, "I LOVE MYSELF!"

Write three of your own affirmations below.

I am _____ !

I am _____ !

I am _____ !

Love yourself today as a virtuous woman!

DAY 5

PRAYING TIME!

Ask God to guide you in becoming the virtuous woman. Ask Him to help you where you are falling short so you may see how wonderful you are in HIM. Write down your prayer.

_____
_____
_____

Week #5

1 Samuel 16:7 (NKJV)
..."do not look at his appearance or at his physical stature... For the Lord does not see as man sees; for man looks at the outward appearance, but the Lord looks at the heart.

TAKING THE TIME

How many times have you noticed people for the way they look and you passed judgment over that person? What was the thought that passed through your mind? Were you being critical or were you being uplifting? Think of how many times you passed by someone and they passed judgment on you. The Bible tells us the only one who can and will pass judgment is our Lord and Savior. What will He pass on you?

Ladies, when you are looking for Mr. Right, don't let his outside appearance be the only thing that attracts you! As Jesus does, look into his heart, and in the process let him see your heart. The outward appearance is more than just the beauty of man; take time to see what is on the inside. As you look inside of someone else, make sure your inward appearance is taken care of. God is the only one that really knows your heart.

As we spend countless hours on our physical being, let's take time to beautify the inside.

WORKBOOK ENTRY #5

DAY 1

Evaluate how much time you spend on your outward appearance per week?

Write down your total of hours. _____

Now evaluate how much time you spend with God per week.

Write your total hours. _____

Compare the times. Do you find yourself spending more time on yourself than with God? Why?

_____

_____

_____

DAY 2

Name five ways you are going to spend more time with God than on your outward appearance.

1.

2.

3.

4.

5.

DAY 3

Congratulations! You are on your way to spending *more* time with God by reading this devotional and completing the questions daily. Write down what you have learned with spending time with God so far.

_____

_____

_____

DAY 4

Your challenge today is to work on not passing judgment on others. For every negative thought you may have about someone, give them a compliment.

Uplift someone who may not be having a good day. Don't pass judgment on their behavior. As you go through the day turning the negative into the positive, write down the reactions of those you come in contact with, blessing them with good conversation and praise.

_____

_____

_____

How has this made you feel to think of others as Christ does?

_____

_____

_____

DAY 5

PRAYING TIME!

Thank you, God, for not seeing us for our outer woman, but for our inner woman. May those around us begin to see their inner woman and see you on the outer. May you use us to let your light shine. Shine, shine, shine. In His glorious name, Amen.

Psalm 90:17 (NKJV)
And let the beauty of the Lord our God be upon us, and establish the work of our hands for us; Yes establish the work of our hands.

TO BE TOUCHED

I can't help but to think that my great aunt who went home to be with the Lord in 2011 was received by the Lord for the works of her hands. She was a very busy woman in her church when it came to doing the work of the Father. She was on several committees and held many important positions in the church. She even made quilts for members of the church and in the community. My great aunt was a true woman of faith and desired to do God's work. I admired her for her countless works and what she believed was work for God's Kingdom. The Scripture that comes to mind when I think of her is, *"Being confident of this, that he who began a good work in you will carry on to completion until the day of Christ Jesus"* (Philippians 1:6, NKJV).

What works have you established to be good? Can you be confident that those works were for kingdom building and not for your own glory?

I encourage you to wash your hands of the earthly things and cleanse them for "righteousness leading to holiness" (Romans 6:19), which will result to eternal life with our Heavenly Father. The Bible tells us that faith without works is dead. It is time to get to work in Kingdom building.

WORKBOOK ENTRY #6

DAY 1

Read the devotional Scripture again and explain it in your own words. Write what this particular Scripture means you.

_____
_____
_____

Describe the works of your hands.

_____
_____
_____

What are your hands doing that is pleasing to God?

_____
_____
_____

DAY 2

Read Romans 6:19

Write down what you understand as the meaning of this Scripture.

_____
_____
_____

What will you wash your hands of in order to do God's work?

_____
_____
_____

DAY 3

What is your role in your church?

_____

If you do not have a role in your church other than being a member, I encourage you to seek the leaders of your church auxiliaries' and find out how you can become a part of that auxiliary/committee.

DAY 4

Describe the importance of Philippians 1:6. What will your good works be?

_____
_____
_____

How will you apply this to your life?

_____

_____

_____

Commit to one of the auxiliaries/committees at your church. Which one will you choose and why?

_____

DAY 5

PRAYING TIME!

Dear God, thank for this time with you. Thank you for my hands and for the things you are about to do with them. Lord, we ask you to help the readers of *Alexandria's Light* to find their places and their roles in their churches just as my great aunt did. May they do it for the uplifting of your Kingdom. May they gain great fulfillment in their church roles. In the precious name of Jesus I pray. Amen and Amen.

Genesis 1:31 (NKJV)
God saw all that he had made, and it was very good.

WHAT DO YOU SEE?

In Genesis 1, the Bible explains all that God created in six days. He created the Heaven and Earth, night and day on the first day (Monday). He created water, sky and dry land on the second day (Tuesday). He created fruit trees and plants for vegetation on the third day (Wednesday). He separated the seasons from the days and years (Thursday). He created the stars for the night on the fifth day (Friday). God united every living thing and every moving thing. He blessed them and said, "Be fruitful and increase in number and fill the seas and let the birds increase on earth" (Genesis 1:22). God created wild animals, livestock, and creatures moving on the ground; God also made man in His image on the sixth day (Saturday).

Can you look back on all the things you have done and declare that everything was good? When you look back at your life, whether it was a day, a year or even a season, was it good? Right now I want you to repeat, "Lord, thank you for making all things good". Recognize that God made it good for you. Realize that He is the beginning and the end. If you have something in your life right now that is not good and you know it's not pleasing to God, ask God right now for forgiveness and ask Him to make everything good, in the name of Jesus.

WORKBOOK ENTRY #7

DAY 1

Imagine the Lord speaking to you about your current situation. At this very moment, would He tell you your situation is good?

Explore your answer.

_____

_____

_____

Would He scold you or pat you on the back? How would you feel about what His answer would be?

_____

_____

_____

DAY 2

In our Scripture the Lord referred to things He completed as *"good"*.

According to Merriam-Webster Dictionary - Good is defined as 1. suitable, fit, 2. free from injury or disease 3. Not depreciated 4. Commercially sound 5. Reliable 6. Profitable, advantageous.

In your own words, write your own definition of *good*.

_____

_____

_____

How does your definition of good make you feel in comparison to what God calls good?

_____

_____

_____

DAY 3

Pick two of the definitions and compare them with your written definition. Are they similar?

Explain why they are or why they are not similar.

_____

_____

_____

DAY 4

Notice in the Scripture, God doesn't say things are bad He said, "and it was good".

Write down a few things you need to fix in your life to make it for the good.

1. _____

2. _____

3. _____

Write down what you have learned from this scripture.

1. _____

2. _____

3. _____

How will you apply it to your life?

_____

_____

_____

DAY 5

PRAYING TIME!

Highlight and repeat the prayer in this week's lesson. Read it out loud with conviction in your heart!

Think about this… God does not make worthless things or people. What God makes is GOOD!

Leviticus 19:4 (NIV)
Do not turn to idols or make gods of cast metal for yourself.

NO NEED TO REMODEL

As women, how many times have we seen a model or an entertainer on television, on the internet, or on the cover of a magazine and said, "I want to look like her"? So we go to our hairdresser and tell them to cut or color our hair like the person we saw. Sometimes, we even take a picture of the individual with us to make sure we get the look just right. Now there is nothing wrong with getting an idea of how a new style can work for you as it did that celebrity; I am talking about when we take it farther than a haircut or hair color. When we decide to go and physically change our own image to look like that other person. God said that we should love ourselves as we are, otherwise we are like an idol. So, it is important that we don't worship things of no value. We should worship our Lord God and not things of this world. We, as women, need to love ourselves for the way we were created and not to look like anyone else. Think about how much money we could save by just being comfortable in our own skin.

WORKBOOK ENTRY #8

DAY 1

What or who do you idolize?

Example: money, men, clothes, shoes, reality television, social media

1.

2.

3.

4.

5.

Explain why you should stop worshipping these idols. How will you put your thoughts into action?

_____

_____

_____

DAY 2

Learn to love yourself. I know you're saying how do I do that? My answer is simple: by accepting yourself for who you really are. Give yourself compliments and mean them. Learn to be comfortable in your own skin. LOVE YOURSELF WITH NO LIMITS. I challenge you to hug yourself and say, "I love myself".

DAY 3

Finish the following statements about yourself. Here are a few to get you started

I AM GREAT because I am a child of the Most High God.
I AM GREAT because I am helpful person to all.
I AM GREAT because I love and respect myself.
I AM GREAT because of my career.
I AM GREAT because I Jesus died on the cross for all my sins.

Your…

I AM GREAT because _____

I AM GREAT because _____

I AM GREAT because _____

I AM GREAT because _____

I AM GREAT because _____

DAY 4

List the things of no value to you other than for material gain in your life.

1. _____

2. _____

3. _____

4. _____

Put a plan into action to start backing away from the things you idolize. Outline the steps. (e.g. I will spend less time on social media, I will not purchase anything new, etc.)

_____

_____

_____

DAY 5

PRAYING TIME!

(You finish this prayer)

All wise God, please help me to start to love myself for who you created me to be. Help me with the things I idolize as I know they are not of you. Empty me with the old and pour into me the new. I no longer want to idolize:

_____

_____

_____

In Jesus' name, I believe and receive, Amen.

Acts 27:34 (NIV)
Now I urge you to take some food. You need it to survive. Not one of you will lose a single hair from his head."

THE ROOT OF THE MATTER

Isn't this good news…to know if we eat food we will not lose one single hair from our head? As I was thinking about the importance of this Scripture, I realized these men were about to be shipwrecked and Paul was encouraging them to eat for their health. I cannot remember how many times my clients came into the salon and pleaded for me to fix their hair because they felt it was "shipwrecked"! It also makes me think of how something as simple as hair, has such a strong hold over us as women and men. Often times, and more than most, our hair is shipwrecked because of poor dietary habits. It is important to have healthy hair.

What we put in our bodies, good and bad, comes out of our pores, including our roots. I ask you to ask the Lord to give you discipline over the foods you shouldn't eat. I encourage you to ask the Lord for deliverance of eating disorders that may be causing you to lose the hair on your head as well as affecting your health. We don't really understand the power our hair and our appearance has over us as women. We all know that if we have a "bad hair day", nothing is really going to go right, so to speak. So remember, whatever you put in your body comes out through your head. Put in good foods and nourishment for your hair and, most importantly, for your body to get the best results.

WORKBOOK ENTRY #9

DAY 1

What do you eat on a normal day?

Breakfast: _____

Lunch: _____

Dinner: _____

Snacks: _____

Ask yourself if you are really hungry when you eat? Are you just eating because it is there?

Do you eat because of the following?

Stress
Boredom
Convenience
Hunger

*CHALLENGE – During this week's devotional, write down all the food you eat each day.

Include the time of day you eat and why you are eating at that particular moment. Is it for nutrition, convenience, stress or out of boredom?

DAY 2

What are the foods you crave?

Write down how these foods make you feel after you eat them.

*Challenge for the week:

Try to limit yourself or remove the foods you crave. Increase your intake of fruits, veggies and protein.

Example – If you like sweet tea, replace it by drinking green tea. If you love cheeseburgers, try removing the cheese and the bun.

DAY 3

Do you realize how important water is for the body? According to President and CEO of Exalted Fitness, Tara Johnson, water helps detoxify the body and hydrate the body; it does wonders for the hair, skin and scalp. Water also helps to maintain balance in bodily fluids.

Now it's your turn, list five benefits of how water helps your body.

1. _____
2. _____
3. _____
4. _____
5. _____

*Challenge for the rest of the week - drink the recommended 64 ounces of water per day. A good trick is trying to drink an 8 ounce glass at the top of every hour.

DAY 4

Ask yourself what steps you will take to become a healthier you? Involve your physician in the process. Make an appointment to meet with a health professional to help you with all you may need to get started on the right track.

Will you:
Push away from the table?
Commit to walking 30 minutes a day?
Add more green and leafy foods to your meals?
Limit your intake on fast foods?
Make a lifestyle change and not just go on a diet?

Write out each step in your plan to get on the path of eating and feeling healthier.

_____
_____
_____

Now that you have a plan, GET STARTED!

DAY 5

PRAYING TIME!

Fill in the blank areas of this prayer and make it personal.

Father, in the name of Jesus, we thank you for this time to be with you on this day. May you help me with the health challenges I face. May you give me the courage and the strength to change my current eating habits and exercise routine. May you bring me to a better understanding of how you want me to take care of my temple. We ask for your healing right now of the following health challenges I am facing:

_____

_____

_____

It is in your name that I ask for revelation to what you want for my life. We believe you will heal and bind up all these things wrong with my body and loose good health over me. In our Healer's name I pray, AMEN!

Week #10

Psalm 139:13-14 (NKJV)

For you formed my inward parts; You covered me in my mother's womb, I will praise You, for I am fearfully and wonderfully made...

ALL PUT TOGETHER

A Masterpiece is what I would call it. God created us in His image in Genesis 1:26 and to conform to the image of His Son Jesus (Romans 8:29). Thank God for thinking so much of us, to create us to be, "fearfully and wonderfully made", in Him. To God be the glory for the Masterpiece He created in you. God loves us, so why do we not feel the same way about ourselves?

When you look in the mirror or at your children, thank God for that masterpiece you see in the mirror. Have your children do the same thing. Teach them to love themselves at an early age.

WORKBOOK ENTRY #10

DAY 1

Imagine you just finished painting your masterpiece. Describe what your masterpiece looks like. Is your masterpiece of your children, your spouse, you dancing with Jesus or of your dream home? Describe how you would feel after the completion of your painting.

_____

_____

_____

DAY 2

Knowing we are God's masterpiece, how would you describe how He felt after He was finished making the earth and all that's in it, Genesis 1:31.

_____

_____

_____

Praise God today for making you from His workmanship and making all our body parts and our inner parts work. Praise Him.

DAY 3

Identify the things you consider to be a masterpiece. Now draw your own masterpiece in the space provided below.

"MY MASTERPIECE"

DAY 4

Write your own personal poem about being fearfully and wonderfully made. I will start it off for you:

> I will praise You Lord for I am fearfully and wonderfully made.
> I will sing praises to you for the workmanship you did in me.
> Look at me, I am God's masterpiece.
> (Your turn)

DAY 5

PRAYING TIME!

Lord we praise your Holy Name. You thought enough of us to make us in your image. Wonderful are your works and amazing are your ways. Lord, we thank you and praise your name, Lord. Amen.

*As you reflect on this week's devotion, take time to look in the mirror and examine the works of God. Take it a step farther and marvel over your children. Take if farther than that. Look at the earth around you and take a moment to appreciate where you live and all that's around it. God is AMAZING in all His ways!

Week #11

John 7:37-38 (NKJV)

If anyone thirsts, let him come to Me and drink. He who believes in Me, as the Scripture has said, out of His heart will flow rivers of living water.

OVERFLOWING

I read this Scripture during a 21-day fast. The fast was for me to get clarity of some life issues and to draw closer to Christ. I read this Scripture and considered many things. My first thought was, *what is the true living water? How does it quench your thirst?* Well, as I read the Scripture the Holy Spirit told me that the living water was not the liquid we drink; it is Jesus Christ - the One who died for all our sins, so that we may have eternal life! All we have to do is seek after Him, obey His word, trust His plan and believe in Him. That's it. And if we do this, we will never thirst again and the living water will overflow from our lives to the lives of others. We can only do this through and by His grace.

Ponder this thought. According to Google, the longest river in the USA is the Missouri River. Imagine how you would drink all the water flowing from this river with the possibility that it would never dry up. This is what the Spirit of the Lord does for us. The living water goes on and on and on. It will never dry up, or run out. This is something to be celebrated and appreciated. As long as we seek after Christ we too will never be dry or run out of His goodness, His kindness, His grace or His Love.

I encourage you to get a drink from the living water, so that you may never thirst again. (Revelation 7:16).

WORKBOOK ENTRY #11

DAY 1

Underline the three active words from the Scripture Jesus said to the people at the festival.

Jesus' instructions were clear. He said, come, drink and believe. Have you followed these specific instructions? Explain.

_____

_____

_____

DAY 2

From Day 1's answer, write what your plans will be to never thirst again.

_____
_____
_____

What will you change or incorporate into your plans?

_____
_____
_____

DAY 3

Re-write this week's Scripture with the words in the word-bank provided.

Thirsty   Blessings   Abundance   Faith

If you are _____ come to me and drink. If you have_____ in me as Scripture has said, out of His heart will come an _____ of _____ .

DAY 4

Re-read the Scripture you wrote and ask yourself this question: What do you need to work on in order to get what the Lord has for you?

_____
_____
_____

DAY 5

PRAYING TIME!

Gracious Father, thank you for your water never running dry. Thank you for your Son Jesus, who has given us permission to never go thirsty again. I will continue to trust and believe in you, Lord. I praise you for allowing your rivers to flow longer and deeper than the Missouri River. I thank you Heavenly Father I will never thirst again because of your darling Son Jesus. It's in His name I give praise. Amen.

Isaiah 61:3 (NKJV)
...to give them beauty for ashes

FROM GRAY TO COLORFUL

No matter what you are going through, no matter what you have gone through, the Lord will turn your circumstances around from a pile of ashes to beauty. Claim the victory while you lay in your ashes and know the beauty of your pain is not far away from those ashes you're in now. You may be going through a tough time right now, but know your tears of sorrow are about to become tears of joy. Believe your sleepless nights are about to be nights of rest. Trust that our God will turn your dark days into days of bright sunshine. Later, you will look back and realize your beauty (circumstances) look better than before and you will realize your ashes have all blown away.

WORKBOOK ENTRY #12

DAY 1

Write down three of the negative things you are dealing with right now.

1.

2.

3.

Write down three positive things you are experiencing right now.

1.

2.

3.

Mediate on your positives and negatives. Turn them over to God by:

1. Praying
2. Fasting
3. Praising

DAY 2

Circle the areas where you need God to turn your ashes into beauty.

Finances   Relationships   Community   Job/Promotion

Health   Church   Children   Education

Why did you choose these particular areas?

_____

_____

_____

DAY 3

From your circled answers in Day 2, prioritize them from the greatest challenges to the least. Write them down.

1.
2.
3.
4.
5.
6.
7.
8.

Now that you have prioritized your list, write one expectation beside each word. If it is freedom, then put that next to your word. If it is peace, then add that next to the word.

DAY 4

Make your word of expectation into a sentence with the word beside it (go back to what you chose in Day 3). Example: I am expecting God to bless me with financial freedom by helping me make a plan to pay off these credit card bills. I believe God to bless me and my family with peace - peace from the storm we are going through at this present time.

Come back in a week or two and examine how God has resolved some of your problems.

DAY 5

PRAYING TIME!

With all the words you have chosen, make a prayer out of them all. At the end of the prayer, add the phrase beauty for ashes, joy instead of mourning, or praise instead of heaviness. Once you have written your prayer out, read it out loud and seal the prayer in Jesus Name. Amen.

_____

_____

_____

_____

_____

Lean over and blow on the ashes from which you have risen.

1 John 4:8 (NLT)
But anyone who does not love does not know God, for God is love.

LOVING FREELY

I have a friend who recently accepted Christ into her life. Before she accepted Christ, she had a hard time making friends or accepting people. She always felt she should keep people at a distance. She said that keeping them at a distance meant she would not have to admit to her own flaws and faults because she was not willing to let people know her as a whole. As a result, she was never able to have a lot of friends. She has expressed to me that if it wasn't for her accepting Jesus Christ as her personal Savior and understanding the love God has for us, she would not know what it truly means or even feels like to love. Now, having Christ in her life she is able to love, but to love freely - knowing and understanding what Jesus did on the Cross for us, a long time ago, is enough.

Love freely today in Jesus Christ, our Lord and Savior. Amen.

WORKBOOK ENTRY #13

DAY 1

One of the definitions of love is: a feeling of strong or constant affection for a person.

In your own words, write your personal definition of "love".

_____

_____

_____

Write down the definition of love from the Scripture. Who is considered "love"?

_____

_____

_____

DAY 2

Read John 3:16. Fill in the blank.

For God so _____ the world so much that He gave His only Son so that anyone who believes in Him shall not perish but have eternal life.

Name five words that describe God's love.

1.
2.
3.
4.
5.

DAY 3

According to this week's Scripture, can you truly love someone if you don't know God? Explain.

_____
_____
_____

Explain what this Scripture means: He who abides in love abides in God and God in Him (John 4:16).

_____
_____
_____

DAY 4

Write out your feelings as to what it means to know Jesus died on the cross for you, so you can have ever lasting life.

_____
_____
_____

How does this change your perspective of His love for you?

_____
_____
_____

DAY 5

PRAYING TIME!

Lord, we know that love is who you are. And we know how much you love us because the selfless act you did for us. You gave your only Son to be born and to die for our transgressions. Even though we are not worthy of this, you still saw fit to do so. Even if we had 10,000 tongues to praise you, it would not be enough. It's because of your unconditional love that we are able to love so freely. And for that we say thank you, God. Thank you for being love and loving us. In Jesus' perfect name. Amen.

Proverbs 3:18 (NLT)

Wisdom is a tree of life to those who embrace her; happy are those who hold her tightly.

IT'S GOOD SENSE

I recently celebrated the sixth anniversary of my mother's death. On February 24, 2009 she went home to be with the Lord. Pancreatic cancer was her demise; she was 58. When I think back just six short years ago it seems like a lifetime. But fast forwarding through these six years, I can say I have made it. It hasn't been easy, but our family has made it.

One thing my mom always taught me and my brother was to be wise. In everything we did, in all our decisions, in the friends we chose in everything - be wise. She would tell us to learn from the wisdom of wise individuals. As I read this Scripture I hear our Heavenly Father saying, "Be wise". In the whole book of Proverbs, God is giving us the instructions to our "tree of life". He instructs us to be wise and not to forget the things He has taught us rather for us to keep His commands. If we obey our Heavenly Father as we do our earthly parents, we will find our reward on earth as it is in Heaven (Matthew 6:10).

I am thankful to God for blessing us with such a wise mother.

WORKBOOK ENTRY #14

DAY 1

Read the following Scriptures listed under each key word from this week's Scripture. Once you read each verse, match the words on the left with the words that best describe the words on the right.

Wisdom – Ecclesiastes 7:12   Tree of Life – Revelation 2:7

Embrace her – Proverbs 4:3   Happy – Proverbs 3:13

Matching:

Wisdom	Blessed
Embrace her	Paradise of God
Tree of Life	Hold on
Happy	Wisdom

DAY 2

Write down your own interpretation of this week's Scripture.

_____

_____

_____

Now think about the kind of guidance you seek from various people - mother, father, friend or co-worker. Who would you consider to give you good godly wisdom? Write their name(s) down and explain why you seek after them for wisdom.

_____

_____

_____

DAY 3

Bless someone today. Take time out of your day to send the individual(s) you mention above an email or text message. Be sure to tell them how much you appreciate them and how much you thank God for them being in your life.

Write down their response to you.

_____

_____

_____

DAY 4

Read Psalm 1:1-3

Verse one tells us exactly what we shall be if we seek after godly counsel. Write down and highlight that one word.

_____

What type of person does this Scripture tell you from who to seek godly guidance (Verse 2)?

_____
_____
_____

Describe what shall happen to a person who seeks godly counsel (Verse 3).

_____
_____
_____

DAY 5

PRAYING TIME!

Write your own prayer and tell God what it means for Him to bless you with such godly counsel in your life.

_____
_____
_____
_____
_____

Romans 8:31-32 (NKJV)
...If God is for us, who can be against us? He who did not spare His own Son, but delivered Him up for us all, how shall He not with Him also freely give us all things?

GIVING FREELY

Doesn't this Scripture make you happy? Doesn't it relieve you to know that God freely gives us all things? All He asks of us is just to believe His Word and His commandments. Believe that Jesus died on the Cross to cover the multitude of sin. All we have to do is accept Christ into our lives as our personal Savior. To do that is easy; the Bible says so in Romans 10:9-10,13 (NLT). If you openly declare that Jesus is Lord and believe in your heart that God raised Him from the dead, you will be saved. As Scripture tells us, "for everyone who calls on the name of the Lord will be saved". In my church this is called, "The Romans Road to Salvation".

I invite you to pray the following prayer to receive Jesus into your life:

Heavenly Father,
I, (your name) receive your Son, Jesus Christ, as my Lord and Savior on (today's date). I know and confess that I am a sinner and ask for you, Father, to forgive me of all my sins and my iniquities against you. I ask, Lord, for your forgiveness of my sins and I repent for all my foolish ways. I believe in my heart your darling Son, Jesus, was crucified and died on the cross at Calvary for my sins. I do believe He got up on that third and appointed day to be raised up to the heavens to be with you. And I know that He is yet alive! Thank you, Lord, for loving me, having patience with me, never giving up on me and for dying for me. Thank you for giving me new life. In Jesus' name, I pray. Amen.

WORKBOOK ENTRY # 15

DAY 1

To whom do you give things freely?

_____

_____

_____

What do they give you in return?

_____

_____

_____

Do you freely give back to God? How?

_____

_____

_____

DAY 2

Underline the word that tells us what God asks us to do in this week's Scripture.

What is the request from God to His people?

_____

_____

_____

DAY 3

Romans 10:9-10 gives us clear directions as to how we are to accept Jesus as our personal Savior. Explain the process:

_____

_____

_____

How did He answer your cry?

_____

_____

_____

DAY 4

Does your church have a "Road to Salvation"?

_____

Have you been down that road?

In your own words declare Jesus as your personal Savior.

DAY 5

PRAYING TIME!

Psalm 18:1-3

I love you, Lord, my strength. The Lord is my rock, my fortress and my deliverer; my God is my rock, in whom I take refuge, my shield and the horn of my salvation, my stronghold. I called to you, Lord, for you are worth of praise, and I have been saved from the hand of my enemy. Amen.

Galatians 2:20 (TLB)
I have been crucified with Christ: and I myself no longer live, but Christ lives in me. And the real life I now have within this body is a result of my trusting in the Son of God, who loved me and gave himself for me.

LAY IT DOWN

The day after my friend invited Christ into her life, I came across Galatians 2:20. I texted her and asked her to read it and tell me what she thought about it. She said, "I was reborn into the body of Christ. My old self has been replaced with the body of Christ". It is amazing to know that she is a new creature and a believer of Christ Jesus. Not only did she accept Christ into her life, but she laid her life down before Him. She laid all of her past life, her fears, past hurts, and her bad habits at the foot of the cross. When she woke up one morning, she called me and said, "I feel great!" She said she slept for 11 hours straight, which she never does. She said she had so much energy that she didn't know what to do with it all. I asked her if she felt free. She gave me the biggest laugh I have ever heard from anyone and said she was released and free! All she did was confess, accept, repent and release. Now, she is experiencing the fruit of the Holy Spirit - love, joy, peace, patience, kindness, goodness, faithfulness, gentleness, self-control (Galatians 5:22- 23 AMP).

Won't you try it? Lay your burdens at His feet today, right this very moment. Cast your cares upon Him (1Peter 5:7).

WORKBOOK ENTRY #16

DAY 1

In your own words, write what this Scripture means to you.

_____
_____
_____

Write down what freedom looks like and feels like to you in Christ.

_____
_____
_____

Lay all your burdens down and leave them with Jesus. What are the burdens you want to lay down?

_____
_____
_____

DAY 2

How will you replace the old with the new as believers in Christ?

_____
_____
_____

Give examples as to how you no longer live for the world, but Christ lives in you now?

_____
_____
_____

DAY 3

Write down what you need God's help with in your life?

_____
_____
_____

What are your plans to trust God?

_____
_____
_____

DAY 4

Like my friend, accept Jesus in your heart. Confess your sins and recommit your life to Christ. What will you say?

_____
_____
_____

Along with my friend, you are now on your way to freedom. Think about how you can help others become free in Christ. How will it sound?

_____

_____

_____

DAY 5

PRAYING TIME!

Oh Lord, how excellent is your name in all the earth. Lord, I come to you on behalf of the readers of *Alexandria's Light* asking that you forgive them of their sins, their past hurts and their bad habits. Lord, we ask you to free them from their fears and free them from the things holding them back from where they have not truly allowed you to live in them. For we know that you are yet alive. We ask you, Lord, for the release of the old things and release a new thing in them. Release love, peace, joy, goodness and rest. Help us to rest in our slumber but, most of all, rest in you. May you place your angels all around each of us to cover and protect us in our new season and in our new skin! We thank you Lord, we lift you on high. We adore you and magnify your Holy Name. In Jesus' name we pray, Amen.

2 Corinthians 4:6 (NLT)
For God, who said, "Let there be light in darkness," has made this light shine in our hearts so we could know the glory of God that is seen in the face of Jesus Christ.

SHINE ON ME

Remember that old saying, "What you do in the dark comes out in the light"? To me, that is what this Scripture says. But I also hear it saying this - no matter how dark your life gets there's always light if you seek after it; the Lord will always shine through if you let Him. He will deliver you, heal you, most importantly, He will forgive you and bring you into the marvelous light through His Son, Jesus Christ. Allow Him to shine in your heart, so you can see the face of Jesus, the Christ. AMEN.

WORKBOOK ENTRY #17

DAY 1

Can you remember a time when you were having a bad day and it seemed like there was nothing you did in that day that made it any better? Explain how you felt on that bad day (being in darkness).

_____

_____

_____

My brother often says, "Today is a great day to be alive". Explain what your "great day is to be alive" looks like (being in light).

_____

_____

_____

DAY 2

When and where do you allow your light to shine?

_____

_____

_____

How do you allow Jesus' light to shine through you, even in difficult times?

_____

_____

_____

DAY 3

Work on coming out of darkness by working on the things that you still struggle with from day to day. Using descriptive words only, name at least 10 of those things.

1.
2.
3.
4.
5.
6.
7.
8.
9.
10.

DAY 4

*CHALLENGE – Search your own heart and from the list from Day 3 turn those dark descriptive words into positive descriptive words. Write your positive words right next to the negative words. Next, describe how the positive words made you feel as you wrote them next to the negative words. The positive words should counter your negative words. After doing this exercise, you should begin to feel a shift as the positive words begin to overpower the negative ones. The words are part of your feelings/emotions. Move your negatives to positives.

DAY 5

PRAYING TIME!

Write your own prayer of deliverance in space provided. Ask God to take you out of darkness, by freeing you from the things you struggle with and to release the light over them. Ask God to search your heart and cleanse it from the things that are not of Him. Make it personal!

_____
_____
_____

1John 4:18 (NKJV)
There is no fear in love; but perfect love casts out fear, because fear involves torment.
But he who fears has not been made perfect in love.

FEAR NO MORE

My brother is eleven years younger than I am. As we were growing up, he would always say to me, "I am not afraid of anything". I just thought because he was a little Dare Devil and a boy is why he would say things like this. Well, as the years have gone by, he still says, "I'm not afraid of anything". Now, as a grown man he still lives by this same motto. But his declaration is, "I refuse to be afraid". I, on the other hand, was always afraid - afraid to spend the night at my friends' and family members' houses or even simple things like go on school trips without my parents. In the early stages of dating my husband, he would always ask me why I was afraid - afraid of everything. As I began to have children, this fear increased. I feared people would harm them if I was not around. I had convinced myself that their own father, my husband, might harm them because he was an only child and was not accustomed to caring for small babies. As the fear increased, I had to make up my mind to increase my relationship with Christ. It wasn't until the death of my mom I decided, NO MORE. Her death made me see life in a whole different light. I realized God has the perfect love, so I just simply prayed to the Lord and asked Him to remove my fear of being afraid. And He has done just that. Now I can love without fear and allow my teenaged sons to live without fear. As they know, their parents love them; they know and also can feel the love of God without fear. Because of His perfect love, now I can honestly say I am not and refuse to be afraid. Amen!

What request(s) do you want to ask God for? Ask, and it will be given to you; seek and you will find; knock, and the door will be opened to you (Matthew 7:7-8).

WORKBOOK ENTRY #18

DAY 1

Admit to all of your fears! List all the fears that torment you.

_____

_____

_____

Now put your fears in order of least to greatest. Explain where the fear originated.

*
*
*
*
*
*

DAY 2

Examine where the root of your fear comes from. Make your requests known to God. Ask Him for what you may need. If it's love, then ask Him for love. If it's forgiveness, then ask him for forgiveness. If it is to remove fear, then ask Him. Write your thoughts here.

_____
_____
_____

DAY 3

Scripture says, there is no fear in love. Ask yourself, are you afraid to love? Yes/No
Explain your answer:

_____
_____
_____

Do you know how to love (without fear)? Yes/No
Explain your answer:

_____
_____
_____

DAY 4

Read 1 John 4:19
Explain this Scripture in your own words.

_____
_____
_____

Find another Scripture in the Bible that tells about God's love. List your Scripture and explain why you choose that particular Scripture.

_____
_____
_____

DAY 5

Using 1 John 4:18-19 and Matthew 7:7-8. Write your prayer request to God. In your prayer, remember God is love.

_____
_____
_____
_____

PRAYING TIME!

Psalm 150 (NIV)

Psalm 150
1 Praise the Lord.
Praise God in his sanctuary;
praise him in his mighty heavens.
2 Praise him for his acts of power;
praise him for his surpassing greatness.
3 Praise him with the sounding of the trumpet,
praise him with the harp and lyre,
4 praise him with timbrel and dancing,
praise him with the strings and pipe,
5 praise him with the clash of cymbals,
praise him with resounding cymbals.
6 Let everything that has breath praise the Lord.
Praise the Lord.

PRAISE HIM WITH EVERYTHING

Saints, learn to praise the Lord. No matter what you are going through, praise the Lord. As His people, we are to praise Him. Praise Him with song, dance, instrument, voice, shouting - whatever you feel comfortable doing. Just praise Him! Today, I praise Him for all the things He has done in my life - my husband and my children's lives and also for my friends. A while ago, my friend called me to tell me she is getting baptized in a few weeks. Not only has she turned her life around, she is going all the way! I just thank the Lord for using me as His tool to spread the Good News (Acts 14:15).
When I asked her how she felt, she said, "At peace". Hallelujah!

Dear Friends,
Whenever you get the opportunity to tell someone about Jesus, be obedient and do so. The reward will be worth far more than keeping it to yourself. I am sure you will be blessed and feel blessed by being a blessing to someone else - another soul saved and brought into the kingdom!
Amen.

WORKBOOK ENTRY #19

DAY 1

Describe how you praise the Lord.

_____

_____

_____

Does your praise look the same at home in your quiet time as it does in church?

_____

_____

_____

DAY 2

Our Scripture tells us all we can do to give God praise. What form of praise do you exhibit?

_____

_____

_____

In verse 6 it says, let everything that has breath praise the Lord, praise the Lord. STOP for just a brief moment and praise the Lord! Turn on your music, sing, clap your hands, stomp your feet, whatever you do, I CHALLENGE you to praise God right now! He is worthy to be praised.

DAY 3

What specific things do you praise God for? List a few.

_____

_____

_____

Do you praise God for others in your life?

_____

_____

_____

Is your praise for real? How so?

_____

_____

_____

DAY 4

How have you allowed God to use you to help advance the kingdom? Give a few examples of this.

_____

_____

_____

Do you still allow God to use you as His tool to spread the Good News of Jesus Christ for the advancement of the Kingdom? Explain.

_____

_____

_____

DAY 5

PRAYING TIME!

It is my prayer for you that you will use anything that was mentioned in this week's Scripture for you to praise the Lord. Do it with your whole heart and remember: LET EVERYTHING THAT HAS BREATH PRAISE THE LORD. AMEN!

Mark 12:30-31 (NLT)
And you must love The Lord with all your heart, all your soul, all your mind, and all your strength. The second is equally important: 'Love your neighbor as yourself' no other commandment is greater than these.

TOTALLY FOCUSED

These are the Lord's Commandments - to Love Him with all our hearts, minds, souls, and strength. As we love Him we are to love His people as well.

If there is someone you are mad at or not speaking to, reach out to that person and show them love - whether it is forgiving them or them forgiving you, work out your differences. In order to love God with everything you have you must first rectify the situation. God can't do a new thing with you or in you, if you are stuck in your old ways.

You must love God first, love your neighbor and love yourself. If you are not able to love yourself, it will be hard to love others.

WORKBOOK ENTRY #20

DAY 1

List anyone you have not communicated with in a while.

1.
2.
3.
4.
5.

Write how you could rectify the situation with them.

1.
2.
3.

DAY 2

If you think there is nothing to rectify, then ask yourself why you have not communicated with that person.

*CHALLENGE – Go and give a neighbor a helping hand. Take time to go and speak to one of your neighbors and see how s/he is doing.

Explain how this challenge went for you. Consider how you responded and how the person responded to you.

_____

_____

_____

DAY 3

How do you love God with all your heart, mind, soul and strength?

_____

_____

_____

Do another random act of kindness and tell someone that God loves them. You never know how these kind words can impact someone's day or life.

DAY 4

Read Mark 4:22.

What happens to the new wine skin if it's put in old wine skin?

_____

_____

_____

How do we allow God to do a new thing in us if we are stuck to things of the flesh? Examples: being mad at people, talking about people, not speaking to your mother, father, brother, sister, best friend, church member, a choir member, etc.

_____

_____

_____

DAY 5

PRAYING TIME!

Father God in Heaven, we give you praise, honor and glory. We ask you to help rectify and mend relationships that are broken. We ask Father that you would mend the homes of family members who are not speaking or who have not talked to one another in weeks or maybe months. We ask you Father to mend bridges for the reasons listed in this week's devotional so you can heal and repair all the things placed in front of you on their behalf. Fix their hearts, minds, and spirits. Give them strength and courage to restore all these things they wrote down and made known to you. In Jesus' name I pray and all the Saints said, "AMEN".

2 Timothy 1:3 & 7, 8 (NKJV)
Verse 3: *I thank God, whom I serve with a pure conscience, as my forefathers did, as without ceasing I remember you in my prayers night and day.*
Verse 7: *For God has not given us a spirit of fear, but of power and of love and sound mind.*
Verse 8: *Therefore do not be ashamed of the testimony of our Lord, nor of me His prisoner, but share with me in the sufferings for the gospel according to the power of God.*

STANDING TRIUMPHANT

When Paul was in prison, he wrote a letter to encourage Timothy to serve God in pure conscience, as our forefathers did, to give testimony about our Lord and not to be ashamed. This is my prayer for all who are believers in Christ.

Today we must declare that we are not ashamed - not ashamed to give God praise, not ashamed to praise Him in our secret places or in public. The Lord said for us to come humbly, but yet boldly so. Not only should we come boldly and humbly, we be bold and unashamed, with no fear, not worrying about what people will say. We must declare in a loud voice the power to speak over the enemy. We must say to the enemy, "We are not ashamed and we are not afraid!" For we know we have victory in God. We know His Word is true in every way because He is the way, the truth, and the life (John 14:6).

It is my prayer for the readers of *Alexandria's Light* if anyone is struggling with life circumstances: fear, doubt, confusion, aches, pains, financial burdens or whoever is just seeking the Lord that they will open up their mouths and pray and leave their problems with God. Nothing is too big for God. So I ask for God to move on your behalf to send the wind in and blow out things that are not of God.

Prayer:
Lord, help these readers to remember you did not give us the spirit of fear, but of power and of love and a sound mind (2Timothy 1:7). Lord, keep them covered in the precious blood of Jesus who died on the Cross for all our sins. This is my prayer in Jesus' name. Amen.

WORKBOOK ENTRY #21

DAY 1

What is your testimony, where God has taken you from "there" to "here"?

_____

_____

_____

Who have you shared your story with in your journey?

_____

_____

_____

Explained how it's helped others. Then consider whose testimony helped you.

_____

_____

_____

DAY 2

The Bible says to pray day and night. How often do you pray?

_____

Ask yourself: Do I pray correctly? If not, then how do I learn to pray more often and more effectively?

_____

_____

_____

DAY 3

Believe it or not, there is a correct way to pray. Many scholars teach people to pray the A.C.T.S prayer. Look up the definition for the understanding of these four words.

1. Adoration
2. Confession
3. Thanksgiving
4. Supplication

DAY 4

Here are biblical terms for these words:

1. Adoration – to praise God
2. Confession – to confess your sins
3. Thanksgiving – to give thanks
4. Supplication – to bring the needs of others and self to the Lord

One of the common prayers prayed that follows the Acrostic Prayer for A.C.T.S. is the Lord's Prayer.

Read this prayer found in Matthew 6:9-13 to get a better understanding of praying.

How has learning this helped you this week in your times of prayer?

_____

_____

_____

DAY 5

PRAYING TIME!

Pray out loud the Lord's Prayer, Matthew 6:9-13.

Week #22

1 Thessalonians 5:16-18 (NIV)

Rejoice always, pray continually, give thanks in all circumstances; for this is God's will for you in Christ Jesus.

NOT JUST TODAY, BUT EVERY DAY

God's will for us is simply to REJOICE - PRAY - GIVE THANKS!

Start off first thing in the morning by doing all of these things. When you spend time with the Master, your day is brighter and clearer. Things that normally bother you…won't. Things that normally get on your nerves…won't.
If you say no more than a simple prayer such as this:

Good morning, Lord! Thank you, God for last night's rest, for waking me up this morning and starting me on my way. It is my prayer, Lord, as I go about this day you will let people see you in me. I pray, Lord, for spiritual eyes, spiritual ears, to be sensitive in knowing when you are speaking to me. Lord, I thank you in advance for today. I thank you for Jesus who suffered, bled and died on the cross for me. I thank you God for freedom which you gave us through Jesus. Because of this, I am free to lift my hands and worship you, free to sing, and free to dance about you and for you. God, thank you for the liberty of no restrictions to praise you. Lord as we go on our day facing life circumstances, I decree and declare this day we shall walk in freedom - freedom in Jesus Christ because you are Emmanuel - God with us. You are God of ALL grace, you are our High Priest and you are Holy and Awesome in all your ways. Thank you, God, for being our Banner - Jehovah Nissi. Thank you, God for being Jehovah Rapha - our Healer and for being Lord of Lords and King of Kings. We thank you for your love, your grace and your mercy. Thank you, God! Amen.

Now that you have said this prayer to begin your day, I challenge you to remember what you prayed when you are confronted with an issue during the day that threatens to steal your joy or your peace. Throughout my career, I have had to learn the importance of putting God at the front of my day is just as important as thanking Him at the end of my day – not just today, but every day.

WORKBOOK ENTRY #22

DAY 1

Try to wake up 30-45 minutes early to start your day off in the Word and with prayer. Commit to doing this 3-5 days a week, then work your way up to 45 minutes to an hour, 7 days a week. If you are not in the habit of doing this already, start with this week's devotional.

Make sure you have a separate journal as mentioned in the Introduction. Give it a name like "My Biblical Discoveries". You will be surprised at your discoveries, but also at how much you grow from one entry to the next.

Journal your time and days and what you experience through this week's quiet time. Include the dates, days of the week, and the time. Notice if there is a pattern that works best for you or if you can hear God more clearly during certain times.

DAY 2

Did the Lord speak to you in your quiet time? What did He say? How did He say it?

_____

_____

_____

DAY 3

What discoveries have you made while you are reading your Bible and spending time with God? Are they about you? Are they about God? Are they even about other people around you?

_____

_____

_____

DAY 4

Where do you notice God speaking to you? (A certain room, a certain place, a certain time of day). Rejoice to God always. Pray and continually give thanks for all things.

Explain why you rejoice.

_____

_____

_____

Explain why you give thanks.

_____

_____

_____

Explain why you constantly pray.

_____

_____

_____

Did you keep your commitment to this week's activity?

_____

DAY 5

PRAYING TIME!

Repeat the prayer in this week's devotional entry.

Write your own prayer down in the space provided.

_____

_____

_____

_____

2 Corinthians 10:3-5 (ESV)

3 For though we walk in the flesh, we are not waging war according to the flesh. 4 For the weapons of our warfare are not of the flesh but have divine power to destroy strongholds. 5 We destroy arguments and every lofty opinion raised against the knowledge of God, and take every thought captive to obey Christ…

BREAKTHROUGH

Breakthrough is coming...the things you used to do you won't anymore. Places you are accustomed to going you won't go anymore. Certain friends and associates you hang with will no longer associate with you. The thoughts you use to have you won't anymore. You have prayed to the Lord to help you. To remove strongholds over your life, whether it is an addiction, family problems, marital problem, unruly children, no food in the refrigerator, a broken down vehicle, or you're without a car, struggling to get ahead or tried of doing things in your own strength. It is time for you to have a BREAKTHROUGH. Don't give in. This is what the devil is hoping you will do. Don't give up. Don't throw in the towel. Don't give the devil that satisfaction. The devil is a lie!

YOUR BREAKTHROUGH IS COMING! Believe it and receive it.

Now I say, raise up your head and hands and say, "Yes" to our God. He is waiting on you. He is the only way. Don't keep Him waiting on you. AMEN.

WORKBOOK ENTRY #23

DAY 1

Strongholds are thoughts we believe to be contrary to the truth - things satan uses to remind us of our past failures and of our sinful ways. He likes to use our emotions to control our mindsets and behaviors. This is a trick of the enemy.

What are the strongholds over your life? What keeps you from breaking free from them?

_____
_____
_____

How have you tried to fix these things in your own strength?

_____

_____

_____

DAY 2

Ephesians Chapter 6 teaches us how to fight against strongholds. According to verse 6:14, fill in the blanks explaining the Armor of God.

Belt of _____

Breastplate of _____

Shoes of _____

Shield of _____

Helmet of _____

Sword of _____ which is _____

DAY 3

Breaking through the strongholds requires your thought process to change. You **must** speak God's Word over your life. Where can you find these Scriptures in the Bible.

- ❖ I CAN DO ALL THINGS THROUGH CHRIST WHO STRENGHTENS ME.
- ❖ I AM MORE THAN A CONQUOR
- ❖ I AM AN HEIR TO THE THRONE OF JESUS CHRIST

What are your Scriptures you use in times of battle? Write down your three choices.

1.
2.
3.

DAY 4

Meditate and memorize this week's Scripture. Use this Scripture to allow it to help strengthen you as you move forward into your breakthrough from the strongholds you are currently dealing with. Rewrite this week's Scripture below. Then say them with power and authority out loud – like you actually believe them.

_____

_____

_____

How will you start to take your thoughts and opinions captive? What is your counter Scripture to your carnal thoughts?

_____

_____

_____

DAY 5

PRAYING TIME!

Father, I decree and declare a breakthrough for ME is on the way. Your Word says to make our requests known. I have confessed with my mouth, my issues and concerns. I am believing God to send an overwhelming blessing and His favor over my life and my family's life. May I see all your works working in my current situation for I know that you are the God of breakthrough. It's in your name I pray, believe and receive your overwhelming, sudden explosion of favor over me and my family. I thank you, Lord, in advance for all that you are about to do in our lives. Amen.

Galatians 1:10 NLT
Obviously, I'm not trying to win the approval of people, but of God. If pleasing people were my goal, I would not be Christ's servant.

MAKING AN OBSERVATION

Let's self-reflect. Can you remember a time when all you wanted to do was please man? You wanted to make sure man was satisfied and man approved of you. But every time we sought after man, we were terribly disappointed - disappointed to the point of being empty, angry or even full of regret and sometimes embarrassment.

Now, let's fast forward to today. Are you still that same person since Christ has entered your life? Paul has told us the brutal truth: Stop pleasing man and be a servant to Christ. If this is something you have tried to do but can't seem to get it right, I encourage you as Paul encouraged the Christians in Galatia who were on the wrong track. If this is speaking to you in any way, like Paul I strongly encourage you to seek God. He will make your paths straight. He will turn your dark days into glorious sunshiny days. God will never disappoint you as man does. He will fill you in all your empty places, He will cover you in the times of a storm. God can do all things, but He certainly never fails. Won't you trust Him? You have nothing to lose; but all to gain - His love, His mercy, grace, and His goodness.

Today, I can personally say I am no longer a "people pleaser". To God be the glory!

WORKBOOK ENTRY #24

DAY 1

Think of a time you put all your trust in (wo)man and s/he disappointed you.

Circle the answers that best fit your feelings:

Mad	Indifferent	Empty
Frustrated	Sick	Regretful
Pleased	Embarrassed	Vengeful

Explain why you chose these specific adjectives.

_____

_____

_____

Name three of your own feelings now.

_____

DAY 2

Now you understand what it feels like when man disappoints you. Explain how you have stopped pleasing man and have started to please God. In your own words, give examples of how this has made you feel. (Remember, it is a process and does not just happen overnight. Pleasing man has been a part of your life since you were young. Now that you are older, it is time to please God).

_____
_____
_____

DAY 3

SEEK GOD ONLY!

Write down 4 steps to get you back on the right track with God.

1.
2.
3.
4.

Which of these steps will you take first?

_____

DAY 4

Read Hebrew 13:8

Write this Scripture out in the space provided.

_____
_____
_____

Explain what this Scripture means to you.

_____
_____
_____

DAY 5

PRAYING TIME!

Based on this week's Scripture, write out your own prayer. Ask and seek God's approval - not man!

_____
_____
_____
_____

Congratulations!

I know God is getting you back on track as we speak. Keep seeking God.

Proverbs: 27:19 (NKJV)
As in water face reflects face, So a man's heart reveals the man.

LOYALTY

This is one of the Scriptures you could hear being said one way and you could read it a totally different way. The first time I read this I had so many thoughts on what it could be but, what matters is what the Lord brought to my attention about the matters of a man's heart being revealed. We never know how someone really is until they get into a situation that causes them to do a hurtful act to the person they say they care about. This Scripture is simply for us to learn not everyone you put in your corner truly has your best interest at heart. I learned once that someone stole some money from someone who she called a "friend", actually her best friend. It was her last bit of money for at least a week before she was to get paid; yet the "friend" did not consider that she would be putting someone else in a bind if she stole the money. It was a hard lesson to learn.

The perfect example of this is Jesus, who told His disciples that the Son of Man would betray Him to the chief priests and to the scribes; and they would condemn Him to death and deliver Him to the Gentiles (Mark 10:33). Jesus even described what they were going to do to Him. He even foretold what He was going to do on the third day (Mark 10:34).

The lesson is difficult, but not complex: just because you are true to yourself and you are loyal to others doesn't mean the "friends" around you feel the same as you do for them or anyone else for that matter. Just because your heart is right doesn't mean others feel the same. What hurts the most about this is getting your heart broken in the process of doing what is right for you or for that person. The pain is unbearable, your heart is heavy and it normally turns into anger, causing you to react in an uncivil manner. **DON'T**.

Remember, all Jesus went through and He still got up on the third day. He didn't go after the ones who betrayed Him. He went on His way. How long will it take you to get back up and go on your way after you have been betrayed?

WORKBOOK ENTRY # 25

DAY 1

Analyze your own heart. What does it reflect when you look into it?

_____

_____

_____

Name 10 things about yourself.

1.
2.
3.
4.
5.
6.
7.
8.
9.
10.

DAY 2

Are you true and loyal to those you call friends? Explain your answer.

_____

_____

_____

What makes you a good friend?

_____

_____

_____

What makes you different than Judas?

_____

_____

_____

DAY 3

Describe your reaction when someone betrayed you. Why did it hurt so much?

_____

_____

_____

Whose actions did your actions resemble?

_____

_____

_____

DAY 4

How long will it take you to get over the betrayal of that person? Have you forgiven them?

_____

_____

_____

What are your plans to move on from your hurt?

_____

_____

_____

DAY 5

PRAYING TIME!

Pray aloud:

Thank you, God, your thoughts are not my thoughts and your ways are not like mine. Cleanse my heart, Lord, and help me to not react to the hurt I was caused by (person' name) and forgive me for my reactions that were not pleasing in your sight. Help me to do as you did when Judas betrayed you. Give me a forgiving heart and a calm spirit. Remove all the hurt, anger and embarrassment I feel from this situation with _____. Teach me to be more like you. Help me to function in forgiveness. May you guide my pathway and make it straight and narrow and not as wide as it has been. I thank you, God, for your giving me another chance t react and behave in a more Christ-like manner. In all things I give you thanks. Amen

Week #26

Songs of Songs 4:7 (NLT)
You are altogether beautiful, my darling, beautiful in every way.

FEELING BEAUTIFUL

Isn't this Scripture romantic? Songs of Solomon is a wonderful love story in the Bible. Ladies, think about how you would react if your man said this to you. First, we would question the compliment and then we would probably ask him if he was feeling ok. I might even say what do you want? Regardless of the reason, we should take this compliment from his heart to ours. Men have a funny way of showing us or telling us how they feel, but when they are being open and honest to us we need to revel in their adoration for us. If you have a hard time accepting his compliments, maybe it's time to do a self-check and figure out why you can't accept what he's saying to you. If your man is telling you how beautiful you are, then you should appreciate the words he is using. Many times we miss what they are saying because we are too busy beating ourselves up for lack of what we don't have or what we don't look like. In order to appreciate them, we must love and appreciate self…first!

For those of you who don't think you're beautiful the way God has created you, then shame on you. Did you forget God made us after Himself (Genesis 1:26)? Learn to love God first, then yourself. If you don't love yourself, you will allow man to do whatever he pleases to you. You will allow him to say whatever he wants to say to you - good or bad. Learn to love you.

I challenge you to take the first step to a better you. If it's losing weight, then find an exercise plan that will work for you. Cut back on your calories. Drink plenty of water. By all means make sure you are current and up-to-date all your annual doctor appointments. Make sure you get all your "girl parts" taken care of (mammogram, Pap smears, thyroid levels, blood work, eye examination, etc.).

If by chance you have no desire or will power to do any of this, just ask the Lord to come into your heart and give you that extra nudge you need to get started. Pray for God to help you get up and moving so that your man can continue to give you many more compliments and, most importantly, so you can feel great about you!!!

WORKBOOK ENTRY #26

DAY 1

What does this Scripture mean to you personally about your husband or boyfriend?

_____
_____
_____

What is your reaction to the compliments he gives you? How would you feel if he didn't compliment you at all?

_____
_____
_____

DAY 2

Let's self-evaluate.

Ask yourself:

Why do you have a hard time accepting his compliments?

_____
_____
_____

Why can't I see myself like he sees me?

_____
_____
_____

DAY 3

Do you love yourself? What will you do to start loving yourself and believing in you?

_____
_____
_____

How can you express love for yourself?

_____

_____

_____

DAY 4

You can start by making sure your doctor visits are current and up-to-date!

When was the last time you went to the gynecologist? _____

When was your last dental cleaning? _____

When was the last time you had blood work done? _____

Ladies that are 35 and older, have you had your annual mammogram? _____

(I say 35 from personal experience. Thank God all went well).

By now, ladies you should have answered the above questions and written your last appointment times in the blanks beside the question. Great job! Pat yourself on the back because you are on your way…

Now, for the ladies that cannot remember their last dates, shame on you...again. Let's make this a priority during this week. Get those appointments made and stick to the scheduled times. This is for your benefit for a long healthy, happy life. It is much easier to love yourself when you know you are taking great care of yourself than when you don't invest on self-care.

DAY 5

PRAYING TIME!

What can you take away from this Scripture?

Genesis 1:26

_____

_____

_____

Write out your own personal prayer. Include the following things:

- ❖ Forgiveness
- ❖ Praise to God
- ❖ Thankfulness for His love
- ❖ Acceptance of self

_____

_____

_____

_____

_____

Dear Lord,

Forgive me for not taking care of the temple you have entrusted to me. Please help me to care for myself as you care for your children. Thank you for your love, Jesus, your kindness and your infinite love for me. Help me to love myself as you have loved me. I know you are not through with your daughters and help us as we work on ourselves and to declare dominion over all things that oppose you. It is in Jesus' name, I do pray. Amen.

Guess what? You're halfway there!

1 Peter 5:7 (NLT)
Give all your worries and cares to God, for He cares about you.

AVOIDING A TRAIN WRECK

As I was doing a client's hair, I noticed how burdened down she was. She came in with a heaviness on her. It seemed as if all the cares of the world were resting on her shoulders. It was so evident, I didn't have to ask what was wrong; it showed. As we discussed what look she was trying to achieve, she began to share with me what was going on in her life. I began to minister to her and I told her exactly what she was looking like as she came in the door. She told me she thought she was going crazy. My client is a retired professional and a very intelligent woman, it amazed me that she really thought she was going crazy. Smh. She contends with all SHE does, all SHE has to put up with, how SHE has to think for her husband, and think for all of the other family members as well. I looked at her and said, "You are not God. Stop playing God. Learn to cast your cares on HIM."

As we went through her hair appointment, she began to realize she was not really any sort of crazy. She realized she was doing everything in her own strength. She thanked me for being honest and she said, "I have forgotten who really takes care of us." I told her sometimes we get off track, but God is a God of many chances. So, get back on track.

If you are reading this, it's not by chance. You were meant to read this. Get back on track. Ask God to search your heart. Ask God to clean up what is messed up. Stop trying to do it in your own strength. Ask for His forgiveness and for Him to put you back on track. Pray Psalm 139.

WORKBOOK ENTRY #27

DAY 1

Write out all your worries, cares, and fears on a separate sheet of paper.

Explain how worrying and being afraid affects your thinking and your daily attitude.

_____

_____

_____

DAY 2

Measure your faith on a scale of 1-10 (1 being the lowest – 10 being the highest). Circle your answer.

1   2   3   4   5   6   7   8   9   10

Explain your level of faith. What practical application will you implement in your life to make your faith stronger?

_____
_____
_____

DAY 3

Recommit yourself back to God. Ask Him for forgiveness. Ask Him to put you back on the right track. How will you get back on track?

_____
_____
_____

DAY 4

Read all of Psalms 139.

How can you apply this Scripture to your life daily?

_____
_____
_____

Rewrite 1 Peter 5:7 and Psalms 139 in your own words, as your own personal Scripture. How will it read?

_____
_____
_____

DAY 5

PRAYING TIME!

Dear Lord,
Please help me to cast my cares on you. When I do, may I leave all of my worries, fears and anxieties at your feet. Wash me, cleanse me, and make me new. Change my walk, my talk and my way of thinking. I am grateful you care so much about me. Amen.

Psalm 139:23-24 (NLT)

Search me, O God and know my heart; test me and know my anxious thoughts. Point out anything in me that offends you, and lead me along the path of everlasting life.

THE MASTER KEY

When I read this Scripture, it reminds me of how merciful God is. This is an actual prayer we can pray. We don't have to try to come up with the right words - it's right there in Scripture – the Psalmist asking God and then giving God permission to show us all our sins and then in return to remind us of them. And then He forgives us of them too. How precious is that? This is the true cleansing power - power to turn everything over to God and be freed…power to have peace from all you are holding on to. Peace leads to your freedom - freedom from bondage and freedom from chains, freedom from strongholds. It's like Grace Williams says in her song, "Your Anointing", God sets you free!

When God's anointing touches me, it sets me free. Ask God for His anointing power. Write down what your freedom looks like. Start off by humbling yourself. In order to do this, you must be honest with yourself. Being honest is not always easy. In order to be freed from all you hold onto, you must come clean. Ask for God's forgiveness (repentance), Confess your faith in Christ and forgive others. Once you have done this, claim your freedom and give God Praise for setting you free. AMEN!

WORKBOOK ENTRY #28

DAY 1

What do the following words mean to you?

Mercy -
Forgiveness -
Freedom -
Peace -

DAY 2

What does your freedom look like to you?

_____
_____
_____

Start living your life today in freedom. What are you holding on to? Completely surrender all your burdens unto the Lord. Confess them all. Now, go!

_____

_____

_____

DAY 3

What sins have you knowingly committed? Consider if you have forgiven yourself.

_____

_____

_____

In what way will you start letting go and begin forgiving yourself?

_____

_____

_____

DAY 4

Allow God's anointing power to free you from all the things you struggle with. Allow Him to set you free. Explain your plan to become free.

_____

_____

_____

DAY 5

PRAYING TIME!

Prayer Works…

Lord, I come humbly before you. Thanking you for spending time with me. It's my prayer Lord that you send your anointing power through the Holy Spirit to fall all over me. Set me free from all the chains I have on me. Touch me, Lord, and release your presence on me. Make me free from bondage, strongholds and from the strong man that lives in me. Your Word says when you set me free, I am free in deed. I lift my hands to you, Lord, for healing, forgiveness, peace and for freedom. I love you and believe in you, God. Extend my faith from mountain to mountain, just like your everlasting love. I honor you, O God, and give you all the praise. In Jesus' name I pray, Amen.

John 8:36 (ESV)
So if the Son sets you free, you will be free indeed.

REDEMPTIVE POWER

Think of a long distance runner winning a race. After he/she crosses the finish line his/her hands are in the air cheering with gladness and victory. The individual has a smile on his/her face that can't be described. That person's heart is beating a thousand beats a minute. Teammates, coaches, parents and fans are all cheering this person on while waiting on the sideline to claim the prize. That's the same exact thing Jesus is doing. Waiting for you to claim the prize – JESUS!

God sent Jesus to set us free from sin - free from satan and his evil ways. Free from calamity, free from disaster, and free from the enslaving powers of sin! Jesus was sent to remove all of that. Although, Jesus does not give us liberty to do what we want, He does give us freedom to follow God.

Jesus can keep us from being enslaved to our sins and He can show us the way to everlasting life. The Bible says that the thief comes to steal, to kill, and to destroy. Jesus said, "I have come that they may have life, and that they may have it more abundantly" John 10:10 (NKJV).

Won't you let Jesus break the power of sin over your life so you can have life more abundantly through Christ Jesus? Can't you see Jesus cheering us on in the race for eternal life with God?

WORKBOOK ENTRY #29

DAY 1

Write out your banner. What do you want it to say at the end of your race?

___

Take your banner of VICTORY, hold it up and wave it around in your house.

DAY 2

How have you claimed the true prize, Jesus?

___

Describe your feeling of knowing that the race has been won in Jesus!

_____

_____

_____

DAY 3

Complete your banner. Write out 10 more banners. What should they say? Use an action word and a description of the area of deliverance.

(Ex: Victory over my enemies, freedom from addiction, etc.)

1.
2.
3.
4.
5.
6.
7.
8.
9.
10.

DAY 4

In your own words, describe John 10:10.

_____

_____

_____

What does your abundance involve? Describe what it looks like.

_____

_____

_____

DAY 5

PRAYING TIME!

Thank you, God, for being my Jehovah Nissi, my banner. You are my banner over my struggles, my strongholds, and all my imperfections. Thank you, God, for cheering me on and waiting on me at the finish line. Thank you, God, for sending your only Son to save me from my sins. I ask you dear Lord to free me from all that is not of you in me. May I learn to walk in your victory and in your peace so that I may have life more abundantly through your son, Jesus the Christ. It is because of Jesus we are all victorious. Thank you, God, for these things in you I pray. Amen.

Hebrews 13:8 (NKJV)
Jesus Christ is the same yesterday, today, and forever.

LIFE CHANGING

One of my clients of 15 years was talking to me and we were discussing the life of our children. She has two young girls in middle and elementary school. My two young men are a freshman in college and our youngest son is a sophomore in high school. She lost her mother a few years before I lost mine and together we have witnessed each other's sorrow, pain and joyful moments. She has been a dear client and a great friend to me and my family.

As I was finishing her hair she said to me "look at how our lives have changed". You have a son that's in college. It wasn't until she said that, I realized how much she was right. My conversation has changed, our vacations have changed, and our household has changed. It's the three of us at home now, while awaiting the arrival of our oldest son to come home on his breaks from college. Now, we are getting our youngest son prepared for the next phase of his life. Not to mention I am writing a book. I call it crazy, life-changing moments. Just like that…in a blink of the eye. But what I find comforting is in knowing that even through all our life changes; Jesus is still the same no matter what. I have even thought about how my life could have been if I didn't accept Jesus in my life. I am so thankful I live in the light and not the dark world of satan.

Aren't you glad in such a changing world we can go to our Heavenly Father who never changes? He is still the same God! He never changes!

WORKBOOK ENTRY #30

DAY 1

How has your life changed in the last six months to a year?

_____

_____

_____

Explain how you have become closer to God in this time or farther away.

_____

_____

_____

_____

DAY 2

How has your household changed during this time?

_____

_____

_____

Explain how the members in your house are closer to God or farther away.

_____

_____

_____

DAY 3

How are your relationships outside of your home? Are they stronger in Christ or do you need to change your circle? (Ex: friends, home environment, church environment, job. etc.)

_____

_____

_____

Concerning your current environment, should you change the location as well?

_____

_____

_____

DAY 4

In our ever-changing life, aren't you glad Jesus is the same yesterday, today and forever more? How has He remained constant in your life?

_____

_____

_____

DAY 5

PRAYING TIME!

Father, in the name of Jesus, we exalt your name, above you there is no other. Thank you for being who you are to me and in my life: my Savior, my Redeemer and my Deliver. I thank you, God, for being the same yesterday, today and forever more. We are living in a world that is always changing, but we find comfort in knowing you are still the same no matter what.

Lord, thank you for your unchanging hands. Thank you for never leaving me or forsaking me. As we go about our days in this forever changing world, may you keep me in your loving arms. Thank you, God, for loving me just the way I am. I give you praise for being the same God all the time. We adore you God our Father. In your sweet Son's name, Jesus, I do pray. Amen.

Esther 4:16 (NKJV)

"Go, gather all the Jews who are present in Shushan, and fast for me; neither eat nor drink for three days, night or day. My maids and I will fast likewise. And so I will go to the king, which is against the law; if I perish, I perish!"

IT'S OKAY TO GRUMBLE

Sometimes praying is not enough. Sometimes we have to fast and pray about our situations, like Esther did. Sometimes we need to shake the heavens and make up our minds that we must fast *and* pray. Jesus fasted for 40 days in the wilderness and was victorious over the devil's schemes (Luke 4:12). The devil could not tempt Jesus.

I have done several different kinds of fasts and all have worked to some degree or another. It wasn't until I did the *Daniel Fast* by Susan Gregory that I saw results from the heavens. This fast has helped me understand what fasting is all about. It was broken down in a way that I could understand the purpose and meaning of what I was trying to achieve. It explained in great detail how to fast with or without food and water. The book explained the kind(s) of fasts to choose – corporate, individual, a partial fast or a whole day fast. My experience through this book was amazing. Not only did I have breakthroughs, I heard the Lord speak to me and tell me things He wanted from me and for me. I had clarity with my thoughts, and even my physical body felt better because I was actually eating healthier. My husband participated in the fast along with me and experienced some amazing things as well.

I encourage anyone who is in need of a closer relationship with God or if you feel your prayers are not being answered just by simply praying, let me encourage you to fast. Fasting will discipline you; it will give you clarity over areas of your life that are cloudy, confused or misunderstood. You will receive breakthroughs and blessings after blessings. If there is a desire for you to fast or if it's been a thought in the back of your mind, won't you try it? You have nothing to lose. Try to start with a half day fast or a 1-3 day fast and build your way up to longer days of fasting. My husband and I have built ourselves up to a 21-day fast. We have learned so much more about each other and about the God we serve. Once, my husband did a fast for 10 days with just water and no food. Talking about powerful! Our pastor has done a 21-day fast with just water. It seems crazy I know, but they were beneficial and well worth the sacrifice. The fast you choose will depend on you and what results you are searching for. Whatever you choose to do for your fast, be clear on the matter. Keep a journal on your progression. And when you start to see what God is doing and the prayers He is answering, be sure to give Him the praise! God loves His children who are obedient and searching for more of Him. If this is for you, go for it. He won't let you fall.

Keep in mind fasting is not the easiest thing to do, but the results are unbelievable.

TO GOD BE THE GLORY!

WORKBOOK ENTRY #31

DAY 1

Why do you feel like your prayers are not being heard?

_____

_____

_____

What do you need clarity on in your life?

_____

_____

_____

Do you need to break the devil's schemes?

_____

_____

_____

DAY 2

*CHALLENGE

Try to do a half day fast for the next 5 days.

Make your request known to God for the desired breakthrough. Record them here.

_____

_____

_____

If you accept this challenge, write out your plan for your fast. Preparation is the key. From what will you do a half-day fast or a full-day fast? Mornings or evenings?

_____

_____

_____

DAY 3

Read the following Scriptures about fasting. The purpose of these particular Scriptures is to give you a better understanding of how people in the Bible did different types of fasts and for different reasons. Which one can you relate to?

Luke 4:1-2

_____
_____
_____

Daniel 10:3

_____
_____
_____

This week's Scripture: Esther 4:16

_____
_____
_____

DAY 4

Write down your Pros verses your Cons in making your decision to fast for your specific needs.

<u>Pros</u>   <u>Cons</u>

Ask yourself; do I really want a closer relationship with Christ? Explain why.

_____
_____
_____

DAY 5

PRAYING TIME!

Lord, as I decide to fast for a cause help me to move closer to you. Help me to understand why you say I must sometimes fast along with praying. Hear my prayers Lord. Spread your favor over me as I attempt this fast to become a better me in you. I trust in You, Lord, that I will be successful in my quest to sacrifice certain things as you did for me. I pray, God, you will see my efforts to become closer to you. May I be victorious in you. Amen.

2 Samuel 22:29 (NIV)
You, Lord, are my lamp; The Lord turns my darkness into light.

HEAVENLY WATTS

Have you ever been alone in the dark? Have you ever walked into a dark room that had no light coming in, like a dark, damp basement? Have you ever been stranded at night outside in the cold? Have you ever answered the phone to find no one on the other end? What about all those days where you have had no sunshine, especially through the winter months? Only dreary days and dreary nights seem to exist.

Well, this is how your life would be without Christ in it. No sunshine, just darkness, no one to answer you on the other end of the phone. No one to text you back…nothing.
Like David, let's praise God and be thankful we have Him in our lives. I know I am! Because of Him we have all we need - His Light and His Love.

WORKBOOK ENTRY # 32

DAY 1

Write down your definition of "The Light of Jesus".

_____

_____

_____

Read the entire chapter of 2 Samuel 22. Write words from the chapter that describe "The Light of God".

_____

_____

_____

DAY 2

Jesus is all we need. Fill in the blanks of each sentence.

2 Samuel 22:3

Jesus my _____, my _____, and my
_____.

2 Samuel 22:26

Jesus is _____.

Jesus is _____.

Jesus is _____.

DAY 3

Explain a situation where God brought you out of darkness into the marvelous light.

_____

_____

_____

What do you currently need to turn over to Jesus for Him to work things out for you?

_____

_____

_____

DAY 4

Name a few people you know that Jesus' light shines through them.

_____

_____

_____

What makes those people mentioned different than the other people in your life?

_____

_____

_____

DAY 5

PRAYING TIME!

*In your quiet time go to God in prayer. Ask God to bring light unto your dark situation.

Father, I'm so glad to know you are my light. I am glad to know you can take me out of darkness and continue to shine your light on me. I praise your name for being my sunshine, my shield, my rock and my deliverer. From this point forward, Lord, I turn over to you all of my problems, struggles, and my insecurities. I no longer want to be in the dark. I want to be brought into the marvelous light. I trust you, Lord, to work it all out for me. In your name I do pray. Amen.

Psalm 96:2 (ESV)
Sing to The Lord, bless his name; tell of his salvation from day to day.

TELL IT!

Think about how news travels. Good news travels fast. As my friend is embracing her new life as a new Christian she has become contagious. Not only has Christ changed her life, He has also changed her husband of 20 years as well. Her spark has ignited the love of Jesus back into his heart and now their household is on fire! This was a household where the husband was christened as a child. He knew about God, but didn't really want to get to know Him. He knew he was going to heaven, but didn't do anything to figure out how he was going to get there. Now it's all they talk about. They have both gone to another level in their lives as Christians. They attend church regularly, their parenting skills have become stronger, and they commit to studying and trying to live their lives by the Word of God, *together*. They are overall inside and out a stronger, happier couple. It's contagious! I tell you, sharing the Good News of Jesus day to day is an awesome experience.

While there is still light in today, I challenge you to share the Good News of Jesus. Let God use you to help someone come to Christ and join my friends in their zeal for the Lord.

WORKBOOK ENTRY #33

DAY 1

Think about how you share your good news. Is it by text, email, a phone call, or maybe through a newspaper announcement?

_____

_____

_____

Now think about how you share the Good News of Jesus Christ?

_____

_____

_____

DAY 2

What relationship do you need God to make stronger?

_____

_____

_____

Name the person(s) and what part of your relationship you would like to become stronger.

1. _____

2. _____

3. _____

DAY 3

*CHALLENGE

Share the Good News of Jesus to one person a day for the rest of this week. Write down how they responded to you sharing your story of Jesus with them.

_____

_____

_____

How was your spirit just as contagious as my friend's spirit?

_____

_____

_____

DAY 4

Read Psalm 39:1. How will you apply this to your life?

_____

_____

_____

Sing praises to the Lord. Write down at least 10 ways you sing His praises.

1.
2.
3.
4.
5.
6.
7.
8.
9.
10.

DAY 5

PRAYING TIME!

Oh Lord, I bless your name. I sing praises to your name for being who you are to me in my life. I thank you for being my Sovereign God. I thank you for your mercy and your grace. As we go about our day, may you allow your light to shine through me so I may be able to share your Good News to someone in need. Decrease me and increase all of you in me so that I can ignite someone's flicker into a flame so that they too can run on just a little while longer. Help me to share the story about a man named Jesus, who walked this earth and died a horrible death, so that we may live and be forgiven of all our sins. Bless us Lord and give us the right words to speak as we share our testimony to the lost. We bless your Holy Name, Father. Thank you in advance for what you are about to do in us all. Thank you. Amen.

Ephesians: 5:33 (KJV)
Nevertheless let every one of you in particular so love his wife even as himself; and the wife see that she reverence her husband.

WORTH THE EFFORT

As I read this Scripture, God revealed my parents' marriage to me. My parents were married for 40 years. They married in their early 20s. They were hard-working people. They worked full-time jobs and owned a janitorial business at night. They never stopped working. I can remember many times going to their cleaning sites and watching them work. They did this five nights a week, side by side. My brother and I were fortunate to grow up in a two-parent home. Seeing my father treat my mom with the utmost respect and my mom honoring my father as her husband, her friend and the head of the house was a blessing. My parents were the best. They were great providers and teachers; they taught us valuable life lessons. They were our biggest supporters! From the passing of our mother, my father really taught us what "until death do us part" really meant. I believe in my heart this is why I am able to love my husband the way I do. This is one of those good learned behaviors.

Just a few days ago I sent my husband a "just because email". I told him how I was thankful for him and what a great father and provider he is. I told him how much I was glad God sent him to me. I even said to him I pray God continues to make me a good wife for him. Quite naturally his response was "thank you" and he said I am a good wife. I can't help but believe this is another great lesson from my parents that God taught them through Scripture. Marriage is not always easy, but if you love yourself and respect others this is a good foundation you can build on day after day, year after year - together.

Look into your marriage/relationship. Make sure you do as the Bible says. Love, respect and honor one another.

WORKBOOK ENTRY #34

DAY 1

What lessons have you learned from your parents or other godly married couples?

_____

_____

_____

Are there any lessons you still stick by from the teachings of your parents/mentors in your adult life?

_____

_____

_____

How do they still help you?

_____

_____

_____

DAY 2

Write three words in this week's entry that describes why the Bible says we should treat God like a marriage. (Hint – answer is in the last sentence of this week's devotion).

_____

_____

_____

In your own thoughts, underline the words that describe God to you from the entry above.

DAY 3

From the words you underlined, write down and explain your choice of words.

_____

_____

_____

How do you apply these words to your relationship now with your husband/significant other?

_____

_____

_____

DAY 4

Email your loved one and send him a "just because email". Print out his response and attach it to Day 4's entry.

Once He responds, write down how it made you feel.

_____

_____

_____

DAY 5

PRAYING TIME!

Father God,
I come thanking you for the marriage of man and woman. It's my prayer that couples all over the world experience the love you ordained in your Word. May the reading of this week's devotional entry help us to see one good side to such a great marriage. May our "just because email" bring joy to our spouses and spark a new thing in our relationships. May the email create dialogue between the union of man and woman. May these couples be blessed all the days of their lives united as one in you and through you. Amen.

2 Corinthians 9: 6-7 (ESV)

6 The point is this: whoever sows sparingly will also reap sparingly, and whoever sows bountifully will also reap bountifully. 7 Each one must give as he has decided in his heart, not reluctantly or under compulsion, for God loves a cheerful giver.

THE SEED CONTRIBUTOR

Just a few days ago, my cousin BLESSED me with a brand new laptop. She told me it was for me to use for my books. I was speechless! She told me she had to do it, as she was being obedient to what God had instructed her to do. I was completely blown away! First, because I would never expect her to purchase such a big item like that for me. Second, because laptops are big ticket items, especially when people have their own financial responsibilities. As she put the box in my hands she spoke blessings over it. She said, "Use it for not only one book, but also for your second one." *Smh…*

What's my point to this? My cousin is a perfect example to this Scripture - not only for me, but for a lot of people. She is a "giver". She has always given to others whether it is giving food, money, time, or a place to live. She has always put others before herself and while she is blessing others she is looking for nothing in return – nothing! This is a "cheerful giver". Her ultimate goal in life is to have money, not for selfish reasons, but to use it for her ministry, which is sowing seeds throughout the land for people. She is the perfect example of what Jesus was doing in the Scriptures in the book of Mark. He fed people, He gave generously to people. He even told His disciples what His true purpose was here on earth. He came to serve and not to be served (Mark 10:45).

We, too, are supposed to be like Jesus. Ask yourself these questions: In what ways am I supposed to be like Jesus? How often am I obedient to what God instructs me to do? If the Lord instructed you to purchase a big ticket item, would you obey?
I am thankful for my cousin, not just because of the gift, but because she is obedient to the Lord. For that I know she will wear her crown in Glory! To the cheerful giver, may God continue to bless you in abundance. Praise be to God!

WORKBOOK ENTRY #35

DAY 1

How do you describe your giving? Is it cheerful or do you do it grudgingly?

_____

_____

_____

Give an example of enjoying the reaping of the good seed(s) that you have sown.

_____

_____

_____

DAY 2

What do you typically give to others? Is it time or is it monetary?

_____

_____

_____

Consider a time when you have had an ugly disposition after you gave a large gift. How did it make you feel?

_____

_____

_____

DAY 3

In your quiet time today, read the book of Mark. Write down some ways you are generous like Jesus?

_____

_____

_____

In what magnitude do you help others?

_____

_____

_____

DAY 4

Are you listening for God's instructions? What has He told you to do, but you have *yet* to do it?

_____

_____

_____

How has the Scripture for this week spoken to you? How do you apply this to your daily life?

_____

_____

_____

DAY 5

PRAYING TIME!

Lord, it is my prayer that you decrease me and my ways and increase your ways in me, so that I may start reaping the good things I sow instead of the worldly things sown. Help me, Lord, to remove me and my selfish ways out of the way of what you are trying to get me to do for you and the uplifting of your Kingdom. When I give Lord, may the receiver see you in me and not my fleshly self. I lift you up, oh God. I magnify you and adore you, Lord, with all my soul. In your Son's name I pray. Amen.

Philippians 4:19 (NIV)
And my God will meet all your needs according to the riches of his glory in Christ Jesus.

THE PROVIDER!

How many times have you gotten down to your last dollar and you didn't know where the next dollar was going to come from? Pay day is at least a few days away and your savings account is empty. Even the coin jar at home has IOUs in it. Even worse, how many times do the kids open the fridge and look in it and say, "I am hungry and there is nothing to eat in the fridge." You are stressed and you can't figure it out. Now is a good time to practice using your words. Now is the perfect time to recite this Scripture and believe it!

There are many times we try to figure out things in our own strength and nothing happens. Haven't you learned by now we have to call on God for Him to help and then we have to let Him do just that? I challenge you to call on God for your situation you are facing right now. God is a provider. His name is JEHOVAH-JIREH for a reason. Whatever you are facing, whatever you are going through I encourage you to use this Scripture. If you don't have any other words to say remember God analyzes your moans and your groans. He is our Author of Faith; won't you put your faith in Him?

WORKBOOK ENTRY #36

DAY 1

What are your struggles?
Circle all that apply.

Finances	Health	The opinions of others
Relationship	Empty refrigerator	Pressures of society
Job/Career	Lack of rest	Finding peace

How does this week's Scripture apply to your life right now?

_____

_____   _____

_____

DAY 2

Learn to speak the opposite of your struggles. From your choices you circled in Day 1, pick 3 and make them positive affirmations. Example: I am not broke. I'm just temporally out of cash.

1.
2.
3.

DAY 3

Read the follow scripture: 2 Corinthians 9:10-13. Explain how this speaks to you?

_____
_____
_____

Declare and Decree this Scripture to yourself and write your own prayer.

_____
_____
_____

DAY 4

If you are a person who thinks God does not hear you when you cry out to Him, think again. Pour your heart out to God and know He will hear your request.

_____
_____
_____

Describe what it means for you to have faith in Jesus Christ who suffered, bled and died on the cross for you?

_____
_____
_____

DAY 5

PRAYING TIME!

Jesus, Jesus, Jesus,

I call on your name for your help. I believe you can help me with all that I'm facing. Lord, please help me in the following areas if my life:

1.
2.
3.
4.
5.

Take away these burdens like I know you can. These struggles are much bigger than me, but I know there is nothing too hard for you, Lord. I thank you Lord because you are the author and finisher of my faith. You did send your Son, Jesus, for me and my sins. I believe you can and will supply all my needs so I leave all my burdens in your hands. I am trusting in you to fix it, Jesus, fix it! In your name I pray, Amen.

John 14:2-3 (NKJV)
2 In My Father's house are many mansions; if it were not so, I would have told you. I go to prepare a place for you.
3 And if I go and prepare a place for you, I will come again and receive you to Myself; that where I am, there you may be also.

ONE-WAY TICKET

Imagine you were preparing to go on a trip – a dream vacation. You called the travel agency and told them what you wanted; they said no worries, leave it all up to us! All we will need from you is the date you plan to take your vacation and the destination and, of course, your payment. They will work out all the other details. Once everything is approved, you are good to go. Pack your bags; you are all set for your vacation spot. They promise to come and get you on the date of your arrival and they also promise to return and pick you up for your departure.

Jesus has to be our ultimate travel agent. He has told us our destination and where we will be staying. He made sure He prepared a place for us and He is also preparing His return. Jesus is so hospitable. Although, we do not know the day or the hour of His return, don't you want to make sure you're ready for your eternal vacation? Jesus came to fulfill the promises of God so that we may have eternal life. Won't you decide on your two destination packages? HEAVEN or HELL. I hope you choose the right package because it will be a one-way ticket.

THINGS TO CONSIDER:
As you would prepare for your vacation, you should prepare for your final resting place.
Do you have a will?
Do you have a living will?
Do you have a burial plot or have you decided to be cremated?
Make sure your house is in order for your final vacation destination.

WORKBOOK ENTRY #37

DAY 1

How is Jesus your ultimate travel agent?

_____
_____
_____

How will you trust Him with all the details for your final destination after life on earth?

_____

_____

_____

DAY 2

How do you prepare for your earthly vacation?

_____

_____

_____

How will you prepare for your eternal vacation?

_____

_____

_____

DAY 3

According to Isaiah 65:11, 17-19

In Heaven there will be rejoicing, joy, no more weeping, and no more crying.

According to Revelation 20:10

In Hell there is fire and brimstone, agony and defeat. Which destination package will you choose, Heaven or Hell?

_____

_____

_____

When you go on vacation you normally take a suitcase. List some items that are in your earthly suitcase:

*Keep in mind these words describe you here on earth.

Circle all that apply:

Wise	Loving	Obedient	Hellish Church Attender		Struggling
Humble	Manipulative	Forgiving	Helpful	Defeated	Overcomer
Helpful	Defeated	Faithful	Trustworthy	Malicious	Kind
Tormented	Deceitful	Truthful	Peacemaker	Sacrificial	Baptized
Worshipper	Shameful	Victorious	Transformed	Vain	Hurt

Put all the words you circled into your earthly suitcase.

```
┌─────────────────────────────────────────┐
│                                         │
│                                         │
│                                         │
│                                         │
└─────────────────────────────────────────┘
```

DAY 4

Set a goal to work on the word(s) you choose in Day 3 that does not line up with God's words.

_____

_____

_____

What do you imagine your destination to be like? Write down your description of Heaven or Hell.

_____

_____

_____

How will you apply this week's verse to the *rest of your life*?

_____

_____

_____

DAY 5

PRAYING TIME!

Heavenly Father, I give you praise for being my ultimate travel agent of my life. I praise you for going before me to prepare a place for me to live eternally. Thank you for incorporating me after life here on earth. Thank you for sending Jesus to die on the cross for us all. I ask you, God, to help me to align the things in my suitcase that are not of you with all the good fruits of yours. As it says in your word, James 4:8: if I draw near to you, you will draw near to me. I thank you for being a gentleman and allowing me to seek after you, O Lord. As I go about my journey, I ask for your traveling mercies. In Jesus Name I do pray, Amen.

Mark 3:3 (NKJV)

And He said to the man who had the withered hand, "step forward."

STEPPING FORWARD

Jesus was in the synagogue when he noticed this man. The Bible says, he watched and he watched him *closely*. Although it was the Sabbath Day, Jesus had to decide what was right - to help or not to help, to heal or not to heal. As He looked around the synagogue He tried asking questions to those who were there. No one answered, so Jesus decided to heal this man. He asked him to stretch out his hand and he did. His hand was restored back like the other hand. The man had a matching set of hands. But all the while this was taking place, there were people in the room who were not happy.

Well, I have news for you - not everybody you are around is going to be happy or excited about your blessings and what the Lord has done for you. SO WHAT! Be like the man with the withered hand, step forward when Jesus calls you. Don't worry about the people to your left or to your right. Continue to keep your eyes on Him. If you know Jesus is calling you to step forward or to move forward in a different direction, be like the man with the withered hand and simply STEP FORWARD. It doesn't matter what your disabilities are - Jesus will fix it. He is not worried about what others say, so why should you? As the song writer wrote for the song, "Moving Forward", I'm not going back, I am moving ahead. Jesus makes all things new and we should all follow Him FORWARD!

WORKBOOK ENTRY #38

DAY 1

What has God called you to do?

_____

_____

_____

What do you need from God to step forward?

_____

_____

_____

DAY 2

In the same way as Jesus had to decide, who are you going to help? Why?

_____

_____

_____

At what cost do you help someone?

_____

_____

_____

DAY 3

How does this Scripture speak to you? How will you apply helping people to your daily life?

_____

_____

_____

Is Jesus calling you in the direction you are currently going in or is he directing your path elsewhere?

_____

_____

_____

God wants to use you, but you're in His way. How will you go about getting out of His way to do a good work in you (Philippians 1: 6)?

_____

_____

_____

DAY 4

Read the following Scriptures. Answer what the Scripture speaks to you?

2 Samuel 22:37

_____
_____
_____

Isaiah 42:16

_____
_____
_____

Proverbs 3:6

_____
_____
_____

DAY 5

PRAYING TIME!

Lord, wherever you go I will follow. Where you lead me I shall not stray from. I am stepping forward, Lord. I want to do as you call me to do. I have decided to move toward your path of righteousness and not by the world's standards. Forgive me for all of my sins and transgressions. I ask for you to help me move forward - not looking back on the past. I do not want to be turned into a pillar of salt like Lot's wife was (Genesis 19:26). I want to move on toward you. In Jesus' name I do pray. Amen.

Deuteronomy 31:6 (NJKV)
Be strong and courageous. Do not fear or be in dread of them, for it is the Lord your God who goes with you. He will not leave you or forsake you.

YOU ARE NOT DEFEATED

It was just the other day when I had this exact Scripture given to me by my husband. I had an appointment that didn't go like I thought it was going to go. I thought I was going to go in to my attorney's office and she was going to tell me when I was going to collect on my inheritance. Well, it clearly didn't go like that. She gave me more "homework" to do. She said for me to go back and find more of my family members who may be owed some of the same inheritance I was entitled to. So immediately I felt defeat! I thought WHY do I have to do all the work and why doesn't GOD just give me what's mine NOW? The other family members aren't putting in leg work, why should I do for them and why should they get ANYTHING? WHY? WHY? WHY? What made it worst for me was I was fasting. So I thought because I was being obedient to the Lord with my fast He would give me my inheritance NOW. This was not the case...

As I left her office (in defeat), I called my husband who didn't answer. So, I waited about 10 seconds and called him back only to get the same, no answer! UGH! So I called a family member who usually picks up when I call and she did. Well, when she said hello I began to weep. I said to her, "What is the point of me fasting and trying to be obedient to the Lord if I have to feel like I'm defeated?" She said to me, "You are not defeated." She started reminding me of the story of Jesus being tempted by the evil one in Matthew 4: 1-11. She also gave me instruction to walk about my inheritance seven times as they walked around the walls of Jericho. What she said to me rang in my ears. She said, "If Jesus was tempted, why do you think you are excluded from that? And if the walls of Jericho came falling down then so will the things standing in the way of your inheritance." As she spoke such "tough love" to me, it woke me up. She then said get your face together and go on to work! So, I did just that - feeling a little better, but not much.

After I hung up with her, my husband called me back about 30 minutes later and I was able to share with him in a more civilized manner than with my family member. He told me not to worry about it and he then emailed me the Scripture above. He didn't get all bent out of shape; he stayed in his calm loving tone and he began to minister to me what God was going to do about this situation. Between the two of them, my husband and my family member I felt a relief. And what I was reminded of is I am not exempt! Just because I am fasting and trying to do the right thing and trying to do what's right for me to acquire my inheritance doesn't me I am exempt from the schemes of the devil. If he did it to Jesus, he certainly will do it to me and to you. The "love of my life", as I call my husband, eased my mind to the point I stopped feeling sad and discouraged.   I am glad I did what I know to do and that's to call on praying, spirit-filled people - Warriors of God is what I like to call them.

When the evil one slips into your mind, call on folk that will pray him out. Don't go around in despair feeling defeated like I left that attorney's office. Although, I knew I was under attack I allowed the devil to use my mind as his playground, but I'm glad I had enough sense to call on my Prayer Warriors. Who are your prayer warriors? When is the last time you called upon them to intercede for you?

WORKBOOK ENTRY #39

DAY 1

Who do you consider to be your prayer warriors?

_____

_____

_____

How often do you call on them and in what kinds of circumstances?

_____

_____

_____

DAY 2

Just like the walls of Jericho, write down the situation you are facing.

_____

_____

_____

Now walk around what you wrote down 7 times.

What will you do to increase your faith in God while you're going through your current situation?

_____

_____

_____

DAY 3

Read Proverbs 3:5. How can you apply this Scripture to your life today?

_____

_____

_____

How will you trust God in your current situation you face today?

_____

_____

_____

DAY 4

Don't allow the devil to use your mind as his playground. Write the opposite word for the words provided below.

Defeat -

Anxious -

Disobedience -

Weeping -

Worry -

How does this week's Scripture speak to you right now?

_____

_____

_____

DAY 5

PRAYING TIME!

Prayer for my readers:

Dear Father in Heaven, I come to you on behalf of the readers of *Alexandria's Light*. Lord, we come to you with thanksgiving on our hearts and with praise on our lips. As we have gone through this devotional for the week we have learned not to feel defeated when obstacles and struggles come our way. We know that the devil doesn't want us to be happy but to feel defeat, anxiousness, to weep, to worry and to be disobedient. We declare right now the opposite of the evil ones schemes. We decree in the name of Jesus you will bless us with your peace, victory and joy. We believe that the devil has no place in our minds and he has no power to play these mind games he tries to play. We claim victory in you, Father, and we believe your word will not come back void. Hallelujah! These things we ask and claim in your darling Son's Jesus Name, Amen.

1Samuel 1:10 (NIV)
In her deep anguish Hannah prayed to the Lord, weeping bitterly.

THE GREAT COUNSELOR

I was watching a televised message and toward the end of the broadcast the preacher began praying for the people in the audience and he started calling out different life issues most people face. As he was led, he started praying out loud to several different areas. He called out the word "depression". As he did this, he asked for women who were suffering from depression to come forward so he could pray for them. While woman were moving fast and in a hurry to the front of the stage, this pierced my heart. I could not believe the amount of women running to the front for prayer. I began to ask the question, *Why*? Why does this illness attack so many women?

I heard The Lord say, *Because they have not come to me. They try to do it in their own strength, they know me and come to me in prayer, but they don't have enough faith in me to heal them from their illness. They need to leave their troubles with me. I AM THE GREAT I AM. I died on the cross for my Father's Children. I now sit at the right hand of God* (Mark 16:19). I have not given to you the spirit of fear, but of power and of love and a sound mind (2Timothy 1:17). Jesus said, "Come to me, all of you who are weary and carry heavy burdens, and I will give you rest" (Matthew11:28). Find rest in me.

Hannah is a perfect example of someone going before the Lord and praying about her problems. Not only was she depressed, she was angry. She was slipping into a depression and she knew it - which is why she went to the tabernacle and began to talk to God. She prayed so hard her husband thought she had been drinking and had become drunk. She was so surprised her husband thought that of her. Hannah let her husband know she was not drunk in any type of way. She told him she was merely pouring out her heart to the Lord about her sorrowful heart. As she poured out her heart to God, He heard her and answered her pray.

Has there ever been a time you prayed like Hannah? What have you prayed for and are you still waiting on an answer? Stop right now and pray to the Lord about the problems you are having. You have done it in your own strength for such a long time. I invite you to close your eyes and begin to speak to the Lord. Tell him all about your troubles. Won't you let Him work it out for you? I believe He can and so should you.

Get your SHOUT OUT while you are in the battle; don't wait until it's over – shout now!

WORKBOOK ENTRY #40

DAY 1

How does each of these Scriptures speak to you?

Mark 16:19

_____
_____
_____

Timothy 1:17

_____
_____
_____

Matthew 11:28

_____
_____
_____

DAY 2

What lead you into depression?

_____
_____
_____

Have you sought professional help?

_____
_____
_____

DAY 3

Look up some Scriptures in God's word to help you regain your positive thinking. Write down at least 3 Scriptures.

1. _____

2. _____

3. _____

Explain why you chose those particular Scriptures.

1. _____

2. _____

3. _____

DAY 4

Write down any other things you need God to handle for you?

_____
_____
_____

How will you leave these struggles with God and believe He will work out the struggles for you?

_____
_____
_____

Measure your "Level of Faith" per the size of the seeds mentioned. Circle which ones applies to your faith level.

Sesame Seed   Mustard Seed

Sunflower Seed   Poppy Seed

*No matter how small the seed learn to trust God to help you through your problems. Trust him like you believe you know him.

DAY 5

PRAYING TIME!

Oh Gracious – Great I Am. Your daughters, _____, are suffering with _____ and they need your help. You see, Lord, they have faith the size of a mustard, sunflower, poppy or sesame seed. (Circle your seed). They just need you to step in and show them why you are the Great I Am. Lord, they have heard of your awesome power through your word, but they need you to show up in their lives right now to help deliver them from themselves and from their problems. Deliver them Lord from the things that are not of you, (depression, suicide or addiction). Place the right people in their lives at this time to help and support them through this. We ask these things through your Son, Jesus our Healer, our Deliverer, our Sustainer. Lord, please send your Holy Spirit to help comfort our dear sisters, who are in need of your comfort. Help them, Dear Jesus, help! In your name I pray, Amen.

Week #41

1 Corinthians 8:6 (NIV)

Yet for us there is (only) one God, the Father. Who is the source of all things and for whom we (have life), And one Lord. Jesus Christ, through and by whom are all things and through and by whom we (ourselves exist).

GOD IS...

As I was on my way to work this morning I was listening to the song "God Is," by the late Rev. James Cleveland. As I was listening I thought "wow" those two words "God is" are powerful. As the song continued to play I tuned into the words and not just the melody. It says, "God is" not God was. So I began to think to myself, He is so much more than we recognize. He is so much more than we give Him credit for. Then I began filling in the blank of what God is to me. I made it as personal as I could. I said:

God is my Savior.

God is my strength.

God is my way maker.

God is my light.

God is my provider.

God is my healer.

God is my friend when no one else is.

God is my EVERYTHING.

At the end of the song the choir sings, "God is my all in all."

What is God to you? Fill in the blank at the end of these two words, "God is____". Complete the sentence and make it personal to you. It may be as simple as one word or you may have a list of things to finish completing the sentence. Whatever you do, make it your own. Make Him your own. God is...

WORKBOOK ENTRY #41

DAY 1

Complete the sentence as many times as you can, God is...

_____

_____

_____

Take time to think about why God is all those things to you. Explain.

_____

_____

_____

DAY 2

Read Exodus 15:2 fill in the blank.

God is…

_____

Write out the following Scriptures.

Numbers 23:19

_____

_____

_____

1 Corinthians 1:9

_____

_____

_____

What do these Scriptures mean to you?

_____

_____

_____

DAY 3

The Scriptures have told us God is good, He is our strength and our salvation. It has taught us that God is faithful.

What is Faith to you? How does it make a difference in your life you live today?

_____

_____

_____

What do you do to gain more faith in Christ?

_____
_____
_____

DAY 4

Scriptures to ponder:

Matthew 19:26

_____
_____
_____

Philippians 4:13

_____
_____
_____

Use them to help you build more faith in Christ.

DAY 5

PRAYING TIME!

Lord, I am thankful you have included me in all of your wonderful works. I do not rest my impossible in man, but all in you. You have been so faithful to me even when I wasn't faithful to you. I thank you, God, for forgiving me of all my short comings. I bless your Holy name God, Amen.

John 10:10 KVJ
The thief cometh not, but for to steal, and to kill and to destroy: I come that they might have life, and that they might have it more abundantly.

SUNSHINY DAYS FILLED WITH THUNDERSTORMS

Picture a spring day with the birds singing, the spring breeze flowing, and the sun shining - what we all would refer to as a beautiful day! That is kind of like we look at life. When things are good in our lives, they are good. But when life changes, becomes a thunderstorm and gets us down, we can't seem to see the sunshine because of the dark clouds. We have a hard time saying, "it's a beautiful day", when it's dark and gloomy outside - just like life. It's hard to say life is good when we are going through a storm. How many times do we walk around thinking we have life all figured out, only to realize life doesn't go as planned or according to our plans? So what our flesh automatically does is to begin to worry and stress - causing our bodies harm. Worrying creates stress and stress causes physical ailments like ulcers, mouth sores, muscle tightness, fatigue, loss of appetite, anger, frustration, and unnecessary arguments with our spouse or loved ones. And to top it off, we lose sleep over stress. We may even begin to have anxiety, which may turn into panic attacks. All the things the devil wants us to feel...

When we feel these things, satan is winning. The scripture tells us what the devil wants to do to us: steal, kill and destroy; but that's not why Jesus was sent to us. A good friend of mine says this, the devil comes not only to steal, but he steals your focus off of God and God's promises. The devil kills our vision, our dreams and our goals. She also said the devil likes to try and destroy what God put into us - our gifts and talents. But we must remember Jesus was sent to us so that we can have life more abundantly. So, why do we feel all of these other things? I'm so glad you asked why. It is because of our carnal selves. It's easy for us to fall into the pit of despair and have the "woe is me" attitude. The flesh takes over and we forget to look to the hills from whence comes our help (Psalm 121:1). Instead, we walk around sad and helpless. Let's learn that DEATH and LIFE are in the power of the tongue (Proverbs 18:21). Start speaking LIFE over your situation. Speak and expect victory!

Activity - speak the lyrics from Dorothy Norwood's song, "Victory Is Mine". The first verse is: *Victory is mine, Victory is mine, Victory today is mine. I told Satan to get the behind me, Victory today is mine. Joy is mine…peace is mine…love is mine…*

WORKBOOK ENTRY #42

DAY 1

What does a spring day look like to you?

_____
_____
_____

Describe your perfect day?

_____
_____
_____

How do you describe a bad day? How do you handle it?

_____
_____
_____

DAY 2

When your plans don't go accordingly, how do you handle it?

_____
_____
_____

How do you handle the stress of day-to-day pressures of life?

_____
_____
_____

DAY 3

What can you do to turn your "woe is me" attitude into a more up tempo, upbeat kind, or positive type of day?

_____

_____

_____

Name a few ways you relieve yourself from stress. (Ex: exercise, reading, shopping, gardening, etc.)

_____

_____

_____

DAY 4

Read 1 John 5:14-15

What does it say to you?

_____

_____

_____

How do you get back to focusing on God and not your problems?

_____

_____

_____

Start speaking life over your stressors, your life conditions.

_____

_____

_____

Explain how this week's Scripture has spoken to you?

_____

_____

_____

DAY 5

PRAYING TIME!

Dear Lord, I come surrendering all things the devil tried to steal, kill and destroy from me. I ask you Lord to forgive me of my self-pity. Forgive me for not looking to you in the time of my despair. I know you are the answer to it all. And to God I give it all over to you. I don't want to stress, worry or cause my body pain and illness. I surrender all to you. You're my all and all. I love you and adore you Lord. I know that through you nothing is impossible. So I claim the victory over all my circumstances I face! I am victorious in you. In all things I give you thanks. Amen.

Proverbs 22:7 (ESV)
The rich rules over the poor and the borrower is the slave of the lender.

BILLS, BILLS, and more BILLS

We have all heard the hit song by Destiny's Child. I don't know about your house, but at my house, "bills" remain an everyday, normal point of discussion. Did you pay this credit card bill? Did you pay the house payment? Did you pay the water bill? Did you give the boys money for their lunch at school? Did you pay the bill for car insurance? Bills, bills, and more bills! I am so sick of bills!

I read a bumper sticker once that said, "I owe, I owe, and it's off to work I go!" Does that ring a bell to you? I have decided I don't want to be a slave anymore to bills. I am at an age where I want to start living my life righteously and that includes getting my finances together so I can be the lender and not the borrower. I am all borrowed out.

I frequently listen to the Dave Ramsey Radio Talk Show and hear how he has helped thousands of people. He calls it "Financial Peace". That is what my family is after, not just because it's the fun thing to do, but because it's the way Christ says we should be. I have cut up many credit cards and have stopped borrowing money from banks and finance companies. I have decided to adopt Dave Ramsey's motto: if you will LIVE LIKE NO ONE ELSE, later you can LIVE like no one else. I would like to suggest you look into one of his books. They are now best sellers because of the way they have empowered people to commit to good stewardship.

I am declaring we will be debt free and believing what God's word says.

Activity: Stop running to the stores to get the latest and greatest; try saving the money. Instead get your bills out and get ready to become debt free. Pray over all your bills and bank account(s) and ask GOD to take care of all your financial needs. Be specific in telling Him what it is you desire. After your prayer, make sure you start to live according to God's plan. He has given us instructions about how we should use the money He blesses us with. Start including the Bible's principles on your journey to becoming debt free. God says it; and it shall be done.

WORKBOOK ENTRY #43

DAY 1

In the space provided lay all your bills and your bank statements out on your table. Organize them from the least to the most expensive. If you run out of room, use additional paper.

1.   6.

2.   7.

3.   8.

4.   9.

5.   10.

Create a budget for yourself. There are many tools available to help you create your budget. I recommend: Dave Ramsey's "Financial Peace" at www.daveramsey.com or Crown Ministries at www.crown.org. Take time out to research which one will work for you.

*Challenge - Check your credit report and work on clearing the discrepancies that are reported.

DAY 2

Read the following Scriptures on money. Start with this week's Scripture and explain how you can relate to the Scriptures.

Proverbs 22:7

_____

_____

_____

Matthew 6:33

_____
_____
_____

Malachi 3:8-10

_____
_____
_____

DAY 3

Saving Money

Proverbs 21:20

_____
_____
_____

Do you have a savings account? Yes/ No

If yes, do you deposit in it regularly? Yes/No

If no, make it a priority to open up a savings account. It could be $5.00 - $100.00. You can choose weekly, monthly or have it automatically deducted per paycheck per pay period.

Come up with 3 ways to start depositing money in your savings account. Here are a few of my ideas:

1. Have a yard sale use that money to pay off a debit. Then you can start saving what your monthly payment would have been from the debit you paid off.
2. Collect the loose chain in your house or car. Deposit that into your savings account.
3. Schedule an amount to come out of your checking account and put it into your savings.

DAY 4

The Bible teaches us the first thing that we are supposed to do is give our *first fruit* to God. Do you tithe regularly? Explain your answer.

_____

_____

_____

If you answered "yes", do you tithe your full 10%?

_____

_____

_____

If your answer is "no", explain what holds you back from tithing?

_____

_____

_____

DAY 5

PRAYING TIME!

As you read 1 Chronicles 29:11-12, use this as your prayer and believe God to do it. Write down what you hear God saying to you from your prayer.

Deuteronomy 4:30 (NKJV)
When you are in distress, and all these things come upon you in the latter days, when you turn to the Lord your God and obey His voice.

WHEN I SPEAK

One morning before I could get my head off of my pillow, I heard the name of my co-worker in my thoughts. My first reaction was to question, *why in the world did I just hear her name?* I don't have any contact with her other than our staff meetings. Anyway, before I tried to pick apart all of what could be the reason I heard her name again; I went right in prayer for her. I simply asked the Lord to cover her - cover her, her family and cover her car as she drove in to work since she drives a pretty good distance to get to work. After I prayed for her, I texted another co-worker that I am close to and asked her to pray for our co-worker as well. She immediately responded to my early morning text with "I shall do so"! So I thought, good I have covered her with another praying woman so she should be good.

As I was getting dressed, I felt an urge to go and see her and pray for her. So when I went to work, I went straight to her office and asked her how she was and how was her family. She said to me, "My family is fine; it's me and my health that are not." I began asking her surface questions like if it was the weather, sinuses or allergies. She said to me, "I'm not sure, but I have been on two rounds of antibiotics and have still no relief." As I was about to ask her if I could pray for her, another co-worker came in and distracted us from our conversation, so I left her office. Well, I couldn't seem to let that rest and I knew God was pushing me and I knew I was on one of His assignments. So I decided to pray for her through email. I sent her a prayer of healing and for clarity in her hearing as this was one of the many things wrong with her. She responded with a simple "thank you." She told me she had been up all night prior to the morning I came to see her and she told me she cried the entire night and that what I did for her reminded her to pray to God. I thought, okay Lord that was it; I have completed your assignment - or so I thought; it was not quite over. This led me to being able to minister to her. She asked me how I knew to come and check on her and to offer prayer. I told her that I heard God speak to me. She asked how does He speak to you and how do you know it's Him speaking? I said to her, His voice is clear. There is no confusion when He speaks to me. I have learned to recognize His voice. She told me she grew up in the church and her family was strong believers in Christ. However, she did not know the last time or if anytime she heard from God. A week had passed and I received a message to call her. When she picked up the telephone, realizing it was me on the other end; she said to me, "I heard His voice! You were right; it was clear - clearer than anything I have ever heard before." She said, "He woke me up out of my sleep to speak to me." I told her that I was glad she had recognized His voice. She was so excited. She went on to tell me all that He said to her. At the end of the conversation she began to thank me for being obedient and taking time to help her. She said, "I know God is there I just didn't think to call on Him in my darkest hour." She told me I had reminded her of how powerful prayer can be.

Just as it says in our Scripture verse, when you are in distress, and all these things come upon you in the latter days, when you turn to the Lord your God and obey His voice, He will speak to you. Not only does He speak to you, He hears your cry, your plea, your distress, He hears it all. Don't forget to incorporate Him into your life. Obey what He tells you to do. You have to be ready when He gives you your God Assignment.

WORKBOOK ENTRY #44

DAY 1

How did this Scripture speak to you?

_____

_____

_____

Identify how God speaks to you.

_____

_____

_____

Does God speak to you only in your quite time or does He speak to you before your feet hit the floor in the morning? Where does God speak to you?

_____

_____

_____

DAY 2

Can you remember the last time you were on a God Assignment? Explain.

_____

_____

_____

What did God instruct you to do? What was the outcome?

_____

_____

_____

Were you obedient to the assignment given?

_____

_____

_____

DAY 3

When was the last time God impressed it upon your heart to pray for someone in need?

_____

_____

_____

How did they respond to your gesture of prayer?

_____

_____

_____

Day 4

*Challenge-

Sit for 5-7 minutes and wait for God to speak to your heart. Do this for the remainder of the week.

What did you hear? Write down your experience for each day you do this.

_____

_____

_____

DAY 5

PRAYING TIME!

Lord, I come asking you for forgiveness of my sins - the sins I remember and the ones I have forgotten. I thank you, God, for the blessings you have bestowed upon me. Lord, I come seeking after you, waiting to hear your voice. It says in John 10:27 that your sheep know your voice. So Lord, as one of your sheep, I am waiting to hear from you. Give me clarity as I read this prayer. Bind up the things that are not of you in my head - things like confusion. Loosen clarity so I will know it's you who is speaking to me. Remove me of my fleshly ways, Lord, so I can hear from your still small voice. May I discern the difference between me and Thee. In your Son Jesus' name I pray, Amen.

James 1:22-24 (NKJV)

22 But be doers of the word, and not hearers only, deceiving yourselves. 23 For if anyone is a hearer of the word and not a doer, he is like a man observing his natural face in a mirror. 24 for he observes himself, goes away, and immediately forgets what kind of man he was.

IT STARTS WITH YOU

How many people do you know like this Scripture depicts? Or is this you? How many times do you hear people say, "As soon as I get right I am going to come to church?" Or "Please pray for me, help me get right"; yet they go back and get into the same old mess they just asked you to pray for them about. These are the kind of people that wear you out! "Pray for me, pray for me…" is what I hear all the time. So I would pray, pray, and pray some more. I would pray for people and come out drained and exhausted. It wasn't until I was in a group bible study listening to others give advice to this one particular person. The same person I always prayed for, that is when this Scripture became so real. She comes in asking for prayer, but goes right back out doing exactly the same things she asked pray for.

How many times have you done this or someone you know has done this? Now is the time to start being more than just hearers of the Word. It is time for all those in their own selves to get out of the way and allow God to fix what they are not big enough to do in their own strength.

Stop looking in the mirror and seeing the natural and leaving the same way we came in. Start by wiping the mirror off and start looking for God in it. Stop saying, "I'm going to" and never do. All the saints can pray for you and continue to pray for you, but it won't be until you stop just hearing what people say to you and do something about it. Start praying for yourself. Get in your secret closet and invite God in to help you.

If this Scripture speaks to you, start doing and not just hearing. I would hate for you to get all the way to judgment day and hear God's reply, "I never knew you. Get away from me, you who break my laws" (Matthew 7:2 NLT). You can't serve two masters. Choose this day to worship the Lord.

WORKBOOK ENTRY #45

DAY 1

According to Scripture, which person are you - the hearer or the doer?

_____

_____

_____

How does this Scripture apply to you and your daily walk with Christ?

_____

_____

_____

DAY 2

Are you the person asking for prayer, but continues your old ways?

_____

_____

_____

What are your strengths?

_____

_____

_____

What are your weaknesses?

_____

_____

_____

DAY 3

Look at yourself in the mirror. Describe the person you see.

_____

_____

_____

Are you pleased with the woman you see?

_____

_____

_____

What will you start to do differently in your walk with Christ?

_____

_____

_____

DAY 4

Read the following Scriptures and write down what they mean to you.

Matthew 6:24

_____

_____

_____

Matthew 7:2

_____

_____

_____

Joshua 24:15

_____

_____

_____

DAY 5

PRAYING TIME!

Father God, help us to be doers of your word and not just hearers of your word. Lord forgive me from all the filth and evil in my life so I may humbly accept your word - the word planted in my heart from you - the same word that has power to save souls. Help me to no longer be just a hearer, but to learn to be a doer as well, so that my face will resemble Christ's and nothing of the world. Remind us Lord what 1John 4:4 says, Greater is He that is in you than he who is in the world. Amen.

Psalm 18:30 (NLT)
God's way is perfect. All the Lord's promises prove true. He is a shield for all who look to him for protection.

LOOKING OUTSIDE YOURSELF

For the last week I have heard the words, "God's promises." I was listening to a sermon on the radio. The pastor preached about God's promises. My pastor spoke about God's promises as well. So I thought, what are all of God's promises to us?

I began to look up on the internet to get some answers. I went to various sites to get answers. What I found out is of all the Bible scholars who argue the point, no one knows for sure. Some say over 3,000, others say over 3,500, and still others believe as much as 8,000 promises. The truth be told, the count is endless - just as His blessings are endless!

God's promises cannot be put into a box. They cannot be given a specific number, because there is none. My dad would say, "There is no mathematical equation to this problem." God is immutable. He does not change (Malachi 3:6). His promises are His promises and He does not deter from what He says.

Now, what we have to remember is that His promises may not just be for us. They can come in existence through our children or our grandchildren. Sometimes it will be from the children we have adopted. I was talking to my cousin who says to me "I just want God to give me what I ask for, just like it says in The Book of James. I have been faithful to Him all my life and I still haven't seen the fruits of my labor." The reason she hasn't seen them is because she is too busy looking into self. We have to look around and notice what God is doing all around us. It will come from other avenues.

I always wanted to be a great track runner, but I quit track too early to figure out if I could be great at it. I always wanted to be a good basketball player, only to find myself sitting on the bench or up in the stands. My husband always wanted to be a pilot, but never knew how to pursue doing that as young man. Now it's through our children that our prayers and God's promises are coming to light. It is the same for my cousin; she and her husband adopted her little girl at birth. She is pursuing the same dream of acting as my cousin wanted to do at a young age, but didn't. If God said it, it shall come to light. He is our Protector (Psalm 91). He is a God of order

(1Corinthians 14:33). He is the Author of our Faith (Hebrews 12:2), the God of Grace (1Peter 5:10) and the God of more than enough.

What have you asked God for? What are His promises to you? If He has not answered them, then figure out where you may have gotten off course. Then get back on course and get back in line. Or just take a look around through your children to see if His promises are coming to pass through them. If God said it, He will do it. Ask yourself what the promises are and then pray about it. God will do it!

Write down 3 of God's promises in the Bible. Let me help you with a few I know: Noah and the flood. God promised that he would not flood the earth again; instead He made a covenant between Him and all living creatures. He promised to send the rainbow from the clouds after the rain to remind us of His promise. (Genesis 6-9) He promises to supply all our needs and He does. (Philippians 4:19) He promises to never leave us or for sake us (Hebrews 13:5) and He hasn't. He is AWESOME and what He does for us all is Perfect! AMEN.

WORKBOOK ENTRY #46

DAY 1

What have you asked God for?

_____
_____
_____

What has God promised you?

_____
_____
_____

What have you promised God?

_____
_____
_____

What has come to fruition?

_____

_____

_____

DAY 2

God keeps His promises to us even if it is through our children. Have you noticed God giving you your promises through your children? What talents and gifts do your children have that you know come from you or your spouse?

_____

_____

_____

How does that make you feel knowing your prayers are still being answered all the way back from your childhood through your own children?

_____

_____

_____

DAY 3

The Word of God is full of His promises to us. Find 3 of your own and write them down. (Don't cheat and use mine. Find your own☺).

1. _____

2. _____

3. _____

Explain how this must make you feel knowing God is still fulfilling His promises to us. Even the things you forgot about, God hasn't forgotten them or you.

_____

_____

_____

DAY 4

When the world says you *can't.* Remember God's promises say different.

How will you incorporate this week's Scripture in your way of thinking?

_____

_____

_____

Name one thing you will work towards from God's promises to you. Will it be going back to school or just simply finishing one of the many projects you have started? *Do tell…*

_____

_____

_____

DAY 5

PRAYING TIME!

God may not come when you want Him, but He is always on time. He is on time with everything, especially the promises He has made through His word. He honors promises on our behalf, while even in all of our mess. God, you are not a God that lies and I am eternally grateful for that. We bless your name, Lord. We lift up Holy Hands to you for being an awesome God. We lift our hands to you for being a merciful God, a gracious God, and for keeping what you say in your word to be true. Lord, I love you. Thank you for all that you do and have done in my life. For all the promises you have fulfilled in our lives – past, present and ones to come. In your name, I pray. Amen.

Psalm 42:7 (NIV)
Deep calls to deep in the roar of your waterfalls: all your waves and breakers have swept over me.

THE PRESSURE OF WAVES

The Psalmist is crying out to God, deep calls to deep! I was listening to my favorite singer, Israel Houghton and New Breed singing their song titled "Deeper." It is a song about desiring God to take you deeper in Him by crying out for God to give us a heart like His. The Psalmist has been hurt and is crying out to God for His help:

All of the troubles of the world are upon me and I am in distress and in anguish. Help Lord Help is what I hear the people say. Help me not feel the stress of life on my shoulders. Help me Lord from sinking into depression. I can't carry all this weight on me anymore. I am drowning. God fix my heart to be more like yours. Fix these heavy burdens.

Depression is real. If you feel like you are slipping into this state, ask God to come into your heart and help you find the proper care for what you are feeling. Think about seeking help.

According to statistics on Depression from the Disease Control Center and Prevention, nine percent of Americans have feelings of hopelessness, despondency, and/or guilt that generates a diagnosis of depression. Women are 70 percent more likely than men are to experience depression during the course of their lifetimes according to National Institute of Mental Health (NIMH). They also report women are more likely to get help than men. And let's not forget about our teenagers; Depression affects them as well. It might be more difficult for them as they may not realize there is a way out. Teenagers are more reluctant to reach for help as they do not always feel comfortable in their surroundings or know what is taking place with them. Do not think that all of the problems they face are small and trivial because they are not. Teenage suicide is prevalent among our youth and it continues to rise in our communities daily. Mothers, please check on your daughters. Aunts, check on your nieces. Grandmothers, check on your granddaughters. Sisters, check on your sisters. Women of God, check on other women.

Please know there are different forms and combinations of Depression. Reach out for help. You don't have to go through this alone. If not taken care of, Depression can possibly lead to suicide or you can do bodily harm to yourself. Check your local listings for a doctor or counselor to speak with.

Even at the end of Psalm 42, the Psalmist still finds hope in God and still gives God praise. Won't you do the same?

WORKBOOK ENTRY #47

DAY 1

Read Psalm 42. Pick out 3 verses that describe the state of depression the Psalmist is in. Write down your 3 verses and explain why you choose those particular verses?

1. _____

2. _____

3. _____

Like the Psalmist, what have you called on God to help you with?

_____
_____
_____

DAY 2

Read the following Scriptures. How can you relate them to your life today?

_____
_____
_____

Psalm 42:7

_____
_____
_____

Psalm 1:1-2

_____
_____
_____

Matthew 11:30

_____
_____
_____

DAY 3

Let's self-evaluate. From the words listed choose the words that best describe your current emotional state today.

The Blues	Burnout	Mental Exhaustion	Merry	Hopelessness
Gleefulness	Contentment	Feeling Low	Sadness	Upbeat
Dejected	Hopeful	Despair	Playful	Excited
Blessed	Perky	Blissfulness	Heaven	Joyousness

Explain your reason for choosing the words you chose.

_____
_____
_____

DAY 4

Do you feel at times God is far away from you like the Psalmist? Do you feel as if you are out of alignment with God or out of his will for your life? Write out your own personal prayer to God. In your prayer ask Him to cleanse, align, restore and to bless you. Like the Psalmist has done.

_____
_____
_____

DAY 5

PRAYING TIME!

Cleanse me O' Lord from_____. Restore me from being deeply _____. I have cried to you Lord and I don't feel you. I can't seem to hear from you. Unclog my hearing so that I can hear from you. Open my eyes so I may see what you are after. Open my mouth and I will sing praises to you all the days of my life. Even in my darkest hour I will remember you and your unfailing love to me. I will put all my hope in you and give you the praise forever more. You are my light and my salvation. You are my safe haven and my protector. You are the source of my laughter and my smile. In you I put all my trust in. I love you Lord. I ask that you will raise up all of this weight and send your angels to encamp all around me. Bless me Lord with your love, your mercy and your grace. It's in your cleansing power, your saving power I do pray AMEN!

Genesis 9:16 (NKJV)
The rainbow shall be in the cloud, and I will look on it to remember the everlasting covenant between God and every living creature of all flesh that is on the earth.

COLORFUL INSIGHTS

God asked. Noah did it.

Now, here was Noah - 600 years old! God gave Noah a great assignment. He instructed Noah to build the Ark. He told Noah to have his sons help him build it. God told Noah He was mad at all the violence and corruption on the earth, so He was about to send a flood to destroy everything. In the story of Noah and the Ark (Genesis Chapter 6-9) and because of Noah's obedience to God, God made a covenant between Noah and every living creature through a visible sign. God said, in the cloud is a sign that He will never flood the earth again. Instead, He will send a rainbow to remind us of this promise generation after generation.

God was extremely pleased with Noah's obedience. Even to this day, God still keeps the covenant He made to Noah. Just think, if Noah didn't follow God's instruction, it would not have affected just Noah and his family; it would have affected us all. Because Noah didn't murmur or complain, God gave him favor that allows us to benefit from it many, many years later.

What is God instructing you to do? Have you started the process of obeying God? Don't you want to be like Noah and obey God? It starts with our obedience, so we must stop fussing and complaining. Stop crying out, but never seeking God. Get the instruction God is trying to give to you. It doesn't matter if the instruction is big or small. What matters is the rainbow that will come at the end, after you follow His instruction. With that rainbow comes great peace and assurance GOD is in control. Get the instruction God has for you. He is waiting to bless you and keep His covenant with you. But be careful...you never know who else may get blessed beside yourself. Not only was Noah blessed, so were his sons and their wives. Even the animals were blessed.

Do what God is prompting you to do. You never know when He will bless you like He did Noah. Don't miss your rainbow. Obey God.

WORKBOOK ENTRY #48

DAY 1

Read this week's Scripture. How does it speak to you?

The rainbow shall be in the cloud, and I will look on it to remember the everlasting covenant between God and every living creature of all flesh that is on the earth.
Genesis 9:16 NKJV

_____

_____

_____

Read Ezekiel 1:28

Explain how this Scripture ties into this week's Scripture. What is the meaning behind this Scripture?

_____

_____

_____

DAY 2

Name a few things God has prompted you to do.

_____

_____

_____

How have you done each of these things?

_____

_____

_____

Have you been obedient or disobedient? Why or why not?

_____

_____

_____

DAY 3

Have you ever thought about how others will be positively affected by your obedience or negatively affected because of your disobedience?

_____

_____

_____

Because of Noah's obedience, his family was able to be blessed. Who will be blessed other than you for you doing the work of God through your obedience?

_____

_____

_____

DAY 4

What was the covenant God kept with Noah?

_____

_____

_____

How does it affect us today? Are we as humans the only people that benefit from this covenant?

_____

_____

_____

DAY 5

PRAYING TIME!

God in Heaven, thank you for keeping your covenant with us to never flood the earth again. We are so blessed to know that you are a God who keeps His promises even when we don't. We thank you God for your everlasting love in Jesus' name. Amen.

Philippians 3:14 (KJV)
I press toward the mark for the prize of the high calling of God in Christ Jesus.

WHY WE MUST REFUEL OUR SPIRITUAL TANK

I was driving down the road one early spring morning on my phone, so engrossed in my conversation that I didn't realize I had missed my exit to get to my destination. Normally, this is no big deal because I just regroup, turn around, and go back in the direction from which I came. Well, the problem with this was I was running out of gas. My husband always gets on me for driving with less than a quarter of a tank of gas. Every time he gets on me I respond with "I know my truck, I'm good." But I knew this time was different. As I read the exit signs, they showed no relief of any sort for 18 miles. I knew my truck was not going to make it that far. I was already pushing my luck. So, I found a median in the road and whipped my truck around while pleading for Jesus to help me. (And, yes, I did a U-turn). As I continued to drive down the road in my state of panic, I noticed the exit I was looking for was just a half mile away. I pulled in to the first gas station I came to. Now at this point I started thanking Jesus for letting me get to the gas station. Before I left the gas station I pulled out my phone to put in the address of my destination, only to learn I was just around the corner from the place. Needless to say, I arrived there a few minutes late, but with a full tank of gas! After I settled myself down I was able to process all I just went through and I thought, *this is what happens when you take your eye off of the prize - JESUS.*

For that short period of time, I lost focus of what I was supposed to be doing, but I continued to press on. Even though my direction was slightly off and even though I was slightly panicking, I didn't quit. I didn't give up on where I was trying to go. I had faith that the Lord would see me through. I called out to Him and He kept me. I pressed on. I also realized just as I was just around the corner from where I needed to be, so is God. He is just around the corner; we just need to look for Him. Seek Him out. I am so thankful for God being a faithful, forgiving God. I know I don't want to take my eyes off of the prize anymore.

What about you? What have you taken your eye off of? Are you going in the direction God has showed you or trying to tell you or is your eye off of the prize? Remember, He is just around the corner if we look for Him. Remember, we are victorious in Christ Jesus! Do not let worldly events take your eyes off of the prize. Press on Saints of God, press on!

WORKBOOK ENTRY #49

DAY 1

What are you pressing towards?

_____

_____

_____

What has taken your eyes off of Jesus?

_____

_____

_____

DAY 2

What is God really calling you to do?

_____

_____

_____

What specific thing can you do to focus on God's calling for your life?

_____

_____

_____

DAY 3

God's power comes from His written and inspired words. What areas of your life do you need God's power for?

_____

_____

_____

How do you plan to receive His power for your needs?

_____

_____

_____

DAY 4

God was waiting on me around the corner. Where do you think God is? Is He around the corner or far away from you? Is He around the corner or is he miles away?

_____

_____

_____

What direction will you go to get to Him? Will it be the wide gate that is broad and leads to destruction or the narrow gate that leads to life, that only a few find (Matthew 7:13-14)?

_____

_____

_____

DAY 5

PRAYING TIME!

Lord God, I thank you for your son, Jesus. I am so glad you made Him our ultimate prize. As I press on through my days, help me not to take my eye off of Him. Allow me to enter into the narrow gates with praise and thanksgiving. In your name I pray, Amen.

Matthew 14:31 (NKJV)
And immediately Jesus stretched out His hand and caught him, and said to him, "O you of little faith, why did you doubt?"

WAVES OF A DIFFERENT MATTER

Doesn't it seem like every time you look around, doubt is on the rise. Doubt is everywhere. It is in our thoughts, in our plans, and even in our daily activities. It comes in our minds and says things like: maybe you should have done it this way. Or maybe you should have worn something different. Doubt also comes in after you have completed a big task or an assignment, and you start to question yourself. The list of doubts goes on and on.

Even when we are minding our own business, the work of the ole clever one comes in and creates more doubt. But no, he is just sitting back waiting on us to fall into his little manipulative ways. Where we say, "Yes, I completed the assignment." The enemy says, "Are you sure? Are you sure it's right? What will people say?" Then you think, I was feeling good about this; I was pumped and excited when I finished the project but now I am not so sure.
Listen to me - SHAKE IT OFF! Shake it off and realize it's the trick of the enemy. REBUKE satan- tell him to back off! He has no place in your mind, body or soul. You're going to have to start speaking the word of God over yourself.

I am more than a conqueror. (Romans 8:37)
I can do all things through Christ who strengthens me. (Philippians 4:13)
If God is for us (me), who can be against us (me). (Romans 8:31)

God called Peter to get out of the boat and to walk out on the water. Although Peter did what Jesus asked him to do in faith, fear and doubt set in and he started to sink. Peter panicked and cried out to the Lord to save him (Matthew 14:29-30).
The Bible says, immediately Jesus stretched out His hand and caught him! Even though Peter had little faith, he still had enough sense to call on the Lord for help.

What we need to do as believers is learn to call on Jesus, so He can grab us and put us back in our boat so we can watch the wind cease.
Oh you of little Faith. Why do you doubt? Stop doubting, saints, and start believing Jesus saves and will take away both fear and doubt in our lives.

WORKBOOK ENTRY #50

DAY 1

Read the story of Jesus walking on water (Matthew 14:22-33).

Write down the reason(s) Peter began to sink after he called on Jesus?

_____

_____

_____

What was Peter's reaction?

_____

_____

_____

DAY 2

In Day 1 we realized Peter called on Jesus to walk with Him on the water because he trusted him and wanted to be with Jesus. When Peter realized what he was doing and he realized how high those winds were, Peter's flesh took over and he became afraid and doubted Jesus. What similar situation can you recall where you called on Jesus and he answered you, but during the process your flesh took over and you became afraid and doubted Jesus?

_____

_____

_____

Jesus said, "O ye of little faith". How did you overcome the fear and doubt?

_____

_____

_____

DAY 3

Do you continue to sink by trying to handle your own problems in your own strength? When you did things your own way, what were the results?

_____

_____

_____

Why do you have little faith? How can Jesus help you?

_____

_____

_____

Explain what happens as the winds begin to rise in your life. How will you react to your raging winds? Will you sink or walk in faith?

_____

_____

_____

DAY 4

Read the following Scriptures about how Jesus saves. Write down what they mean to you.

Luke 19:10

_____

_____

_____

Acts 16:31

_____

_____

_____

Romans 10:13

_____

_____

_____

What will you allow Jesus to save you from?

_____

_____

_____

DAY 5

PRAYING TIME!

Father, in the name of Jesus, I ask you to give me the courage to walk on water as you gave Peter. Even though the winds are up against me, may I never sink. Stretch out your hand to me as you did Peter. Save me, Lord, even with my little faith. You say all I have to have is faith the size of a mustard seed. I decree and declare you to make these strong winds calm in my life. I will worship you as our true and living Son of God! Amen.

Galatians 6:9 (NLT)
So let's not get tired of doing what is good. At just the right time we will reap a harvest of blessing if we don't give up.

HOLD ON, HELP IS ON THE WAY!

Are you tired? Are you broken? Are you frustrated? Do you feel as though God is not hearing your cry? If this is you or even a part of you, let me encourage you to hold on, your help from God is on its way! Your harvest is coming. While you are waiting on your harvest to come, you should do a self-evaluation. Pray and ask God to show you what it is you may need to work on for self in order to reap the harvest. You may need to incorporate fasting or spending more time with God - intentionally. You may need to clean out some things in order for God to do a new thing in you.

It's just like a farmer; he has to get his land prepared before he can plant his seeds. He has to make sure to till the ground and smooth out the rough patches in the ground before he can plant the seeds for his crop. Getting up early before the rooster crows is what the farmer does to get things in order. What about you? What are you doing to get your field in order? Once the farmer completes his task for his harvest, he continues to cultivate his land. He does not just sit around and wait day in and day out, he continues to work. He does not give up. He believes he will reap a harvest for his hard work and efforts.

What are you believing God for? Are you like the farmer or are you just a person that sits by and says, should I, could I, would I? What is the seed you are trying to plant for your harvest? Are you looking for a new job or career? If this is what you want, then start by asking God for it? Then begin packing up your personal items at your current job and begin the process of moving. I'm sure you have started applying for other positions at this point, but if you haven't, begin now. If you need a new car, then start the process now. Begin to look into the options you may need to weigh your options and begin to put the act into motion. If you want to purchase a home, whether it's your first time purchasing a home or your second or third time purchasing a home Prepare now! Start with saving money for a down payment. Check with a lender and get pre-approved. Start house hunting. Do the things necessary to reap from your harvest. Learn what the Bible says, seek the ways of God. This way you will be able to find out more about the harvest from God. Psalm 37: 3-4 says, *Trust in the Lord, and do good; Dwell in the land, and feed on His faithfulness. Delight yourself also in the Lord, And He shall give you the desires of your heart.* Know this, children of God. God is a merciful God. He will do what He says according to His word, but you have to put in the time and do some work with God in order to get all He has promised. Do the things necessary so you can reap from the harvest God has for you. Amen.

WORKBOOK ENTRY #51

DAY 1

What seeds are you sowing in order to reap the harvest from God?

_____

_____

_____

What do you need to work on, personally, in your order to reap your harvest?

_____

_____

_____

What old things do I need to clean out of my life in order for God to do a new thing in me?

_____

_____

_____

DAY 2

What are the desires of your heart?

_____

_____

_____

What is your plan of action to get the process started toward your harvest?

_____

_____

_____

How will you prepare for the harvest?

_____

_____

_____

DAY 3

By now you should be motivated and excited about what you are about to sow and what you are about to reap. How do you feel knowing your harvest is starting to come together?

_____

_____

_____

What are some of the things that have come to pass for you so far?

_____

_____

_____

DAY 4

Read Galatians 6: 7-10

What are the good things you have done for others? Name a few.

_____

_____

_____

When you do things for others, examine if it was for selfish gain or merely to help them? Have you reaped anything you have sown?

_____

_____

_____

Give a praise report of what God has done or is doing for you now.

_____

_____

_____

DAY 5

PRAYING TIME!

Lord, I am trying to do good. I am trying to help family members and friends become better Christians and better people in general. I am trying to sow good things so that I might reap good things in order for my harvest to be plenty and good. I know your Word says to do good even when I don't feel like it, which is at times hard, especially in my frustrated, tired, and weary days. You said in your Word not to give up so, I am trying my best not to. As I seek after you, I can't help but to ask, when O God, when are you going to show up and show out? When is the harvest coming? Lord when will it be my season for _____, when? I know it won't be when I say; I know it will be on time as you are an on time God. So, I wait…trusting and believing in you to bless me with my inheritance of a good harvest. As I wait Lord, fix what needs to be fixed: my mind, my attitude, my heart and anything that is not of you and doesn't line up with your will for my life. Restore me, Lord, as I wait on you. I will continue to be good and do good for others, even when I am weary, tired and frustrated. I trust you God. I love you and I will not give up! I wait on you, Father. It is in your name I do pray, Amen.

Jeremiah 33:3 (ESV)
Call to me and I will answer you, and will tell you great and hidden things that you have not known.

THE CALL

What is God calling you to do? What has He been instructing you to do for Him? How many times has He tried to use you as His vessel and you did not answer Him? When was the last time you accepted His calling by answering, "Yes, Lord?" In the Scripture the Lord tells Jeremiah to call to Him and He will tell you great things hidden and things unknown to him. My thought was, if God calls me, will I answer? Will I be like the Scripture that says let your yes be yes and your no be no. As that Scripture teaches us, we should not be indecisive. It says for us to say "Yes" or to say "No". The Bible also tells us not to be lukewarm; it clearly says to be hot or cold. What is our Creator calling you to do? It doesn't matter the size of the calling. What matters is your acceptance.

I started writing this devotional in July of 2012. Through the years, I would pick it up, dabble a bit, and put it back down. I would go and write other things, get halfway through them only to find myself drawn right back to this devotional you are now reading. I questioned God several times as to why He wanted me to write, particularly, a devotional book. I would say things like, "I am not a good writer." "I can't spell half the words I say at times, let alone write it in a book for others to read." I said this to the Lord because this is a very important job. Then more questions followed, "Are you sure I'm the one to do this? Are you sure you want to use me like this for your people? Are you sure you want them to read something I wrote? I'm not smart enough, God. I am only a hairdresser by trade. What could I possibly have to offer to your people? Why are you choosing me, God, to fill such a large order?"

God's response to me was, *Begin to write my daughter. You used to write as a little girl in your adolescent years and you do it now. You have always been a writer; you just weren't hearing me - my voice. I am the one who directed you to the pen and paper. I am the one who taught you how to scrapbook before others made it popular. Now, I am calling you to write about me! To let the people know that even the simple, the meek can minister to my people. Look at Amos. Look at his life, he was by far not dumb, he was not weak in his job or position and neither are you! As I instructed him to do, he did and look how he touched the lives of others. I used people like you and like Amos the meek and the humble. Just accept what I have called you to do so you can help my children. What is the main job of a hairdresser?* He asked. I answered, *"To touch the lives of others through beauty - to touch the lives of others and to empower them to look and feel good". That's what you are still going to do. Your ministry is to get this book in the hands of my daughters. You will introduce them to me or remind them who I AM. You don't have to have a PhD. You just have to listen to me and accept my calling. You just have to trust me and believe I know what I am doing for you and for the lives of others. The Great Commission is to love and you are to remind people of that. Although, it may be a process, you can help them return to me or become closer to me. You will deliver them and you will help set the captives free. You will help the lost find their way back to me. You will help those who have questions find their answers and bring them back to me. This is so they can find rest in me and so they can find joy in me, as well as my peace.*

Christian Family, I have accepted my calling. When will you accept yours? God is waiting for you, say "Yes" and "Amen" (2 Corinthians 1:20).

The Lord does speak to you. He may speak to you directly or through others. He even speaks through His signs and wonders. You just need to learn His voice. Be still long enough to listen for His voice. Develop a quiet time to spend in His word and His presence. Proverbs says: *mediate on His word both day and night.* Genesis says, *God speaks to us in the cool of the morning.* Learn when He speaks to you. Is Jesus calling you? Or maybe he has texted you However, He is giving you His instruction; answer His call. Reply to the text with a definite "yes"!

Here's a thought - instead of always making your request known to God, challenge yourself to ask Him what are His requests from you? Then answer the call!

Be BLESSED!

WORKBOOK ENTRY #52

DAY 1

How does this week's Scripture speak to you? (Jeremiah 33:3)

_____

_____

_____

How will you answer God's call like Jeremiah did?

_____

_____

_____

DAY 2

How will you start to recondition yourself to let your "yes be yes" and your "no be no"?

_____

_____

_____

What is God requesting from you for him? Listen for God's reply.

_____

_____

_____

DAY 3

What have you been dabbling in that you can't seem to turn loose?

_____

_____

_____

What have you decided you will allow God to use you for? What assignment do you seem to be drawn back to?

_____

_____

_____

How will you implement God's plans for your life?

_____

_____

_____

DAY 4

In previous weeks, I have given you the challenge to sit and be still in God's presence. How long do you sit with God now?

Challenge: Write down specific times from this week's lesson, the time you have spent with God. Describe what it was like now versus the beginning of this devotional.

Sunday _____

Monday _____

Tuesday _____

Wednesday _____

Thursday _____

Friday _____

Saturday _____

By now you are a year into this devotional. You should have developed some really good habits that you are committed to in thought, word and deed.

1. Spending quiet time with God.
2. Reading of God's Word daily.
3. Praying to God consistently.
4. Praising Him more – in good times and bad times.

Revisit this yearlong devotional and write down what you have discovered and learned during the course of this year. Write down some things that helped you. Write down some of the things you have overcome and things you may still need to work on. List them below. Remember, you are a work in progress.

*
*
*
*
*
*
*
*
*
*
*

DAY 5

PRAYING TIME!

Lord, I hear you calling me and I say, "Yes". Be with me, Lord, as I answer your call to do what you have gifted me to do. Give me ears to hear and eyes to see your plans for me. Let me do your will, Lord, in the way you would have me to do it. Bind up all of the negative things that come my way, my thoughts and the ways of the world that may create more doubt and fear. Bind other negative thoughts that the enemy uses to distract me like I am not capable or qualified to do what you are asking me to do. Loose from heaven the equipment I need to fulfill your assignment. Loose over me clarity over my mind and confidence in you as I travel along the way. Loose over me peace in my heart and soul. Help my "yes" to be a yes to you Lord. Yes to your will. Yes to your way. May I not bend to the things that may get me distracted, discouraged, and out of the will of you God including the people, the places and the things not of you. Lord, I ask you to use me for the uplifting of your kingdom and to be able to serve in the capacity you want. May you decrease me and increase more of you in me for your work. It is in Jesus' name I pray and give it all over to you, Father. In your name I do pray, Amen.

NOTE TO THE READERS

May the Lord bless the readers of *Alexandria's Light*, and may God use your light to bless others.

Made in the USA
Charleston, SC
08 November 2015